Sunday Dinners

Sunday Dinners

FOOD, FAMILY, AND FAITH FROM OUR FAVORITE PASTORS

{ DIANE COWEN }

FOREWORD BY VICTORIA OSTEEN
PHOTOGRAPHY BY MICHAEL PAULSEN

Andrews McMeel Publishing, LLC

Kansas City · Sydney · London

Andrews McMeel Publishing, LLC
an Andrews McMeel Universal company
1130 Walnut Street, Kansas City, Missouri 64106

www.andrewsmcmeel.com

13 14 15 16 17 TEN 10 9 8 7 6 5 4 3 2 1

ISBN: 978-1-4494-2710-8

Library of Congress Control Number: 2012954410

Photography by Michael Paulsen
Design by Holly Ogden

Attention: Schools and Businesses
Andrews McMeel books are available at quantity discounts with
bulk purchase for educational, business, or sales promotional use.
For information, please e-mail the Andrews McMeel Publishing
Special Sales Department: specialsales@amuniversal.com

Contents

CONTENTS

Foreword

When you stop to think about the bounty of food that God provided on this earth for us to experience, it is truly amazing. The incredible array of tastes, colors, textures, and scents tells me that food is meant to be enjoyed and celebrated. And there is no better way to enjoy God's abundance than to share a meal together with people you love. From the beginning of time, there have been few things that knit us more closely together as humans than to sit down and share a meal. In fact, numerous studies have shown that the more regularly families eat together, the healthier, happier, and better off they are.

Some of my most treasured memories as a child were those times we shared eating together as a family. I can remember the wonderful aromas coming from the kitchen when my mother and father were cooking. Years later, I can still appreciate how coming together regularly over dinner allowed our family to stay informed about one another's daily lives, to talk about our dreams and aspirations, and to just be together.

Joel and I continue that tradition today with our family. On Sunday evenings and on special occasions, it is not unusual for lots of people to gather at our house; parents, brothers, sisters, nieces, nephews, and friends. Of course, there is always lots of food. I believe this is the way God intended food to be enjoyed—together with those you love.

At Lakewood, we teach about taking time to invest in our families and our relationships. That's why I am so glad that Diane decided to write this beautiful book about the tradition of Sunday dinner. I encourage you to share this book with your family. If you don't have a tradition of having meals together, why not start now by setting aside one day a week to sit down to dinner together? Try the recipes in this book, and make it a time to give thanks for your family, friends, and the bounty of food that God provided.

Victoria Osteen

LAKEWOOD CHURCH, CO-PASTOR

Introduction

I've always enjoyed entertaining at home, but one Sunday brunch I prepared for friends several years ago set the pace for what has become a tradition among a close circle of friends—five couples, actually—who have become my second family in Houston.

We'd all gotten busy with family, work, and travel, and hadn't gotten together as a group in some time. As we compared schedules it became clear that a Friday- or Saturday-night dinner out couldn't happen for a while. Sunday became the go-to date, and because one husband in the group leaves town each Sunday evening for business, brunch was the obvious option.

With a date penciled in, I began planning my menu. During the week, I'm all about convenience for lunch and dinner, but on weekends—and when I entertain—everything has to be fresh and made from scratch. I planned a huge meal with baked French toast (my mother-in-law's recipe), cheese grits (a recipe from a former co-worker), quiche (a recipe clipped from the *Houston Chronicle*), biscuits (thank you, Martha Stewart), sausage, and bacon. Friends each brought a dish: fruit, pastries, and more entrées and side dishes.

We gave thanks for our good fortune—good health, great jobs, excellent relationships—and sat down to eat. We talked, laughed, recounted stories from our week, and looked ahead. A game of Trivial Pursuit shifted us from the dining room into the living room and lasted for a couple of hours. We always play it women vs. men, and while I don't remember who won that first game, I do recall that the room was filled with laughter and conversation.

By this time, most brunches would end with everyone saying their good-byes and getting on with their day. But no one said good-bye; no one left. A few gravitated outdoors to sit on our lakeside deck. The rest of us stayed indoors, out of the humidity. By now the huge spread of food was completely gone and a few people were hinting loudly about an afternoon snack. I pulled together some appetizers, set out cheese and crackers, and cracked open a couple of bottles of wine. I still laugh when I think about how quickly the snack round was eaten, especially after the huge brunch.

A couple of hours later, I said to one of my friends, "Unless people start heading home, I'm going to have to make dinner!" Dinner? Just the mention of the word had several people asking what we were going to have . . . and just one suggesting we make a big pot of gumbo and a pan of corn bread. I looked through my pantry, fridge, and freezer and had almost everything we needed. Someone made a run to the supermarket for a few missing ingredients and my kitchen helpers got busy.

By the time it was all over, my friends had been at my home—eating, talking, and laughing almost nonstop—for ten hours. After the last couple pulled out of the driveway, my husband examined the kitchen and declared, "It looks like locusts have been through here!" It was my best party ever.

I've had dinner parties to mark birthdays and anniversaries, as well as cookouts for holidays and themed parties for opening night of Major League Baseball season (Go, Astros!). They're always fun and no one ever goes home hungry, but none has lived up to the legend of that brunch. Every family and group of friends has that legendary party, I think. When you get the right mix of close-knit people, it almost doesn't matter what meal you've prepared. The love comes through in both the food and the conversation.

The same warmth and sense of tradition existed in my childhood in Indiana. My parents took my sisters Cindy and Patty and me to Sunday morning services at a United Methodist Church where we were members. After church we'd go to the nearby drugstore so my dad could buy the Sunday newspaper, and then we'd go home for dinner and an afternoon together. Sometimes we'd pile into the car and drive to the next county over, where my grandparents, aunts, uncles, and cousins lived. We'd visit my dad's mother first and then go down the street to the home of my mom's mother. (Their fathers had died many years before.) If we had time, we'd stop at my uncle's farm. We were city girls and life on a farm, with big tractors, loud, smelly animals, and a nearby woods and creek were an adventure.

Sometimes we'd stay near home, though, and a special treat was to have lunch at Frisch's Big Boy. The restaurant is no longer there, but the chain still exists in the Midwest. I almost always ordered spaghetti and fresh strawberry pie loaded with whipped cream. Strawberries were my favorite food then, and I couldn't resist them in any form. Of course, I was just a little girl and could never finish a slice of pie after a plate of spaghetti. I'm pretty sure my dad let me order the pie because he knew I'd be stuffed after a few bites, and he'd get to polish off the rest.

Both of my parents have passed away, but these childhood memories are strong. I was raised in a Christian family, so church was a given, but the rest of Sunday wasn't necessarily religious or spiritual. But, without question, Sundays were the day we focused on being a family and staying connected to extended family in other cities. I understood it as a child, and now, as an adult, it's even more important to me. I'm not the little girl in the backseat of the car. I'm a wife who wants to have a loving marriage. I'm a sister who wants to stay in touch. I'm an aunt who wants nieces and nephews to think of me as a positive role model. I'm a friend who wants others to realize that life is better because we're in it together.

My career in newspapers took me away from my hometown of Lafayette, Indiana, shortly after graduation from Purdue University. My first job took me to the *Shelbyville News* in the small town of Shelbyville, Indiana, for four years. From there I moved to northern Indiana to work at the *South Bend Tribune* for another twelve years. There I made many friends, learned much about myself as a person and as a journalist, and met my husband, Steve Cowen, whose family is much like my own. A few times, we've even combined the two families for massive dinners at Thanksgiving, Christmas, or Easter. Their big family meals—when everyone was in town—also were on Sundays, and it wasn't unusual for them to include four generations, from great-grandkids to great-grandparents. Now that my husband and I have moved to Texas, a brother-in-law lives in California, and my husband's parents split their time between Michigan and Florida, big family dinners are special occasions.

When the *Houston Chronicle*, the nation's sixth-largest newspaper, offered me a job as a features editor, it was an incredible career opportunity that meant moving to a dynamic and diverse city with a thriving culture. I've done many things at the *Chronicle* and now oversee its religion and food sections. It's a strange combination, to be sure, but it works for me. Usually I write about other people and how they live their faith or how their culture or families unite around the kitchen table. Now, I get to tell you not only how it plays out in my own life, but also how it plays out in the lives of so many others. Hopefully you'll be inspired to consider how you live (or want to live) your own faith and come together with your own family or community.

In this book, I want to introduce you to families you may have heard of but haven't heard enough about. They're pastors at some of America's most notable churches, and they want you to know what happens in their homes.

This book was born from personal experience and extended into my contacts as religion and food editor at the *Houston Chronicle*. The more I think about these two topics, the more I see what they have in common, rather than how different they are: We are enriched by both, one meal and one prayer at a time. The connection seemed like a good springboard for a cookbook for people of faith.

In my job I have the pleasure of meeting interesting and exciting public figures such as Pastors Joel and Victoria Osteen, Rev. Dr. Ed and Jo Beth Young, or Bishop T. D. and Serita Jakes. Through this book I've gotten to know many more, families I hope you'll feel connected to as you read about them. I admire them not just for their successes in the pulpit and in their communities, but also for the strong families they have built. They preach it, and they live it, and that's something to emulate.

I hope they inspire you to use a Sunday afternoon very soon for your own brunch or dinner. If your extended family is scattered, start small with immediate family or close friends. If relatives are across town or a short drive away, pick up the phone and invite them over. If daily life leaves you feeling stressed out and overworked, use this day to slow down and appreciate the good things in your life, whatever they are. You'll create positive memories and stronger connections as you build your own family traditions.

CHAPTER ONE

When It Comes to

Family,

Just Being Together Goes a Long Way

My brother-in-law, Mickey Rigdon, makes living his faith look effortless. He is an earnest man, raised on Midwestern values of humility, hard work, and love of family.

Tall and strong, he is a man who works with his hands. In his thirties, he spent a few years playing semipro football in his hometown of Lafayette, Indiana. As a child, he had athletic ability, but his family was too poor to pay the fees to play football or any other sport or outfit him with a uniform and equipment. So when, as an adult, he saw an ad for tryouts for the Lafayette Lions, he decided to give it a try. Week after week, he took a beating on the field and took no small amount of ribbing from the other guys on the team for being one of the oldest guys to suit up, but he loved it.

His parents had married young and had three boys, Mickey being the eldest. Then his father was in a horrific car accident that left him disabled and barely able to speak. Not only was Mickey Sr. unable to work, his wife couldn't, either, because of the constant care he required. They got by on occasional short-term jobs, government assistance, and the kindness of others at their close-knit church.

"When I was a boy we always prayed at mealtime," Mickey recalled. "At a certain age my brothers and I had to participate. My parents taught us that the main concept was to be thankful for what we had. I don't recall any of the prayers or what they were about, but I do remember that we always were thankful for the food—because that was about all we had," he laughed.

When he was a freshman at Purdue University he met my younger sister, Patty. They married not long after, and a few years later their son, Blake, was born. Several years and a few miscarriages later, the young couple settled in for life with one child. So it was a pleasant surprise when they learned Patty was pregnant again. With only grandsons on both sides of the family, Patty learned she was expecting a little girl.

Six months into the pregnancy, Patty's water broke. She spent the next month or so hospitalized. Childbirth was a scheduled C-section, and excited grandparents-to-be, siblings, and nieces and nephews gathered in the hospital's waiting room. This newborn girl was a happy miracle, so the roomful of smiling faces was stunned when Mickey came from the operating room looking shaken. Patty's heart had stopped, and as doctors revived her with defibrillators she began to hemorrhage. Her heart stopped again. She was revived again. Little Mickaela, weighing less than five pounds, had barely made it out of her mother's womb alive and would spend weeks hooked up to life-saving machines.

The day had begun with happy anticipation. It ended with desperation. We prayed openly in the waiting room, in hallways, in the church chapel, asking God to let both mother and daughter make it through first one night, and then another, and another.

"I'm a strong person, and I think I am because of my faith," Patty said years later. "Mickaela is here by the grace of God. Someday I'll learn why we had to go through that. I think tough times are there sometimes to help us develop into who we are."

As they raised Blake and Mickaela their goals were simple: to instill the same values, faith, and traditions that they were taught; to be caring and thoughtful; to be generous with whatever they have; and to live with open hearts.

Both Patty and Mickey pray often; their prayers are words of thanks. The only "asking" they seem to do is for the good health and safety of loved ones. While their children's sports schedules may have meant that not every family dinner is a home-cooked meal, they're shared around a table nonetheless. And each begins with the four holding hands and saying grace.

"As a father I pray for my kids, their health and safety. Now that Blake and his friends are in college and elsewhere, they're heavy on our hearts," Mickey said.

Mealtime isn't the only time they pray. Conversations with God are ongoing for both. Mickey simply believes that making himself strong spiritually will make him a better person—a good husband and father. Patty finds her drive to work to be her most consistent time alone and often uses that time for meditation.

"Sometimes if I'm having a good day, I thank God for what I have," she said. "Many people pray to ask for things. I like to thank Him every day for the things I have: a good home, healthy kids, a good dog."

Another trial came for the family one summer afternoon when the house next door to their home caught fire. Flames spread quickly; soon their home, too, was engulfed in flames. Blake, sixteen then, was home by himself. He managed to get the family's two Labrador retrievers out and then grab family photos from the living room.

As firefighters aimed high-pressure hoses at their home, the family stood on the sidewalk, surrounded by neighbors and friends who'd heard the news and headed over. Patty and Mickey had on the clothes they'd worn to work. Blake was in shorts and a T-shirt, barefoot. Mickaela had been swimming in a neighbor's pool so she was in her swimsuit, dripping wet. Every other thing they had owned was lost.

In the days that followed, family, friends, and church members began a seemingly endless parade of visits and phone calls. One family had just moved out of their home and into a new one. They offered their vacant home as temporary lodging. Cars pulled up all day long with used furniture, household items, and clothes—enough to get them by until they could settle with their insurance company and move into a new home.

So on a hot summer Sunday evening, the four found themselves in someone else's nearly empty home, sitting on folding chairs around a card table holding a casserole that had been dropped off earlier in the day. Just as they'd done every other day of their lives, they grasped one another's hands, bowed their heads, and thanked the Lord for all that they had: a caring community, cherished friends, and one another.

❧

For my sister and her family, dinners together are sacred. Whether it's a carry-out pizza or a carefully prepared meal, they are always shared around a table. And they're done with intentionality: conversation is a way Patty and Mickey stay plugged in to their children's lives; it's how parents continue to be role models for how children should behave.

Family dinners, of course, aren't limited to everyday meals we eat at home. There are birthdays and anniversaries, holidays and reunions. Some families gather so regularly that they don't require invitations: siblings, cousins, aunts, and grandparents simply know where and when to report for Sunday brunch or dinner—and everyone plays a role.

In my husband's family, spring and summer holidays such as Mother's Day and the Fourth of July meant family matriarch Eldora Cleland was back at home in Indiana from her winter sojourn to Florida. At these gatherings, she was the queen of the kitchen and the three generations that followed were her culinary acolytes. Until she died at the age of ninety-three, she was unfailingly kind, upbeat, and devoted to her family. No matter what else had been prepared for any dinner, Eldora's cooking was legendary. Her fried chicken and chicken and noodles can't be matched, and it wasn't uncommon for her to single-handedly prepare an eight-course meal—everything from scratch—even at the age of ninety.

After plates of comfort food were devoured, the table was cleared and the kitchen cleaned. Decks of cards made their appearance, and that's when the real fun began. The Cowens are a card-playing family, and euchre is their game of choice. With two or three decks of cards and up to ten people around the table, the games can be raucous. They're traditionally played "boys" against "girls" and last for hours, with the boys accusing the girls of "table talk" and the girls accusing the boys of, well, anything we can think of.

When the children, grandchildren, and great-grandchildren in the family remember these get-togethers, what they remember most is the fun they had. Siblings bond over a great hand. In-laws gain acceptance into the family by their ability to hoard that last trump card to the final play of any hand. For other families, the games might be Scrabble, dominos, or even Trivial Pursuit. Others head outdoors to toss a football, splash in a pool, or simply sit and talk under the shade of a sprawling oak tree. It's all the makings of family traditions and memories that are shared and retold year after year.

෴

When generations sit down over a meal, family elders have a chance to help children and young adults see what can lie ahead by understanding their family's history. For the youngest children, there are manners to be learned and common courtesies such as sharing and learning to say "please" and "thank you." Simple, but seemingly vanishing from many children's social skills. When the meal begins with a humble prayer of thanks, parents can encourage empathy, selflessness, trust, and other positive values.

No, Sunday dinners aren't just a check mark on the good-parent scorecard. They must mean something. Conversation takes the gathering to the high ground it should seek. If you think teens and younger children aren't interested, think again. Plenty of surveys report that not only are teens interested in spending time with you, they're paying close attention to what you say and do.

Emily Feinstein, policy research associate at the National Center on Addiction and Substance Abuse at Columbia University, said the center's annual survey has polled Americans' attitudes on family dinners since 1996. The numbers have held consistently at around 60 percent of families saying they eat dinner together at least five times a week. They turn off the TV, banish cell phones and PDAs from the room, and do something incredibly old-fashioned for about a half-hour: they talk. They check in on school, work, hobbies, athletics, and friends. Each question, asked with care and without judgment, takes parents one more step into the lives of their children. And, most important, parents must listen to what their children have to say.

"We love to say that the magic of a family dinner isn't what's on the table, it's what happens around the table," Feinstein said. "Kids tell us, number one, that it's about checking in and talking to their parents. We understand that it's important to parents that they check in with their kids, but it's important to their teenagers as well."

CASAColumbia is known for its research on addiction and substance abuse prevention, but more than a decade ago, its staff decided to add what they call "The Importance of Family Dinners" survey. They ask simple questions about whether families eat together. If not, why? As you might guess, most are busy working or taking kids to sporting events and other activities. A good number simply don't make the effort even though three of five teens who don't have regular family dinners say they wish they did.

"Our research and other research shows that family dinners themselves have value, but a lot of the positive effect really has to do with the quality of the relationship in the family. That's what we talk about with parental engagement: being involved in your children's lives and establishing expectations," Feinstein said.

The best news CASAColumbia's survey delivers is that in families that make the time to have dinner together, the teenagers have zeroed in on the value of togetherness. Some 54 percent say the best part of family dinners is the conversation: talking about their lives and connecting with parents, siblings, and any other family members or friends who are there. What more could a parent want?

Feinstein noted, "It's important for parents to remember that in imparting values and expectations, they're teaching children what the limits should be and that children will live up to their expectations if parents are firm and clear about what they are."

D. Michael Lindsay, the current president of Gordon College and a former Rice University sociologist whose area of expertise is how religion intersects with family life, agreed with the CASAColumbia survey. "There are plenty of surveys that indicate—regardless of whether they want you to know it—teens are paying very close attention to how adults live their lives," Lindsay said. Do you want them to be compassionate and caring, honest, and hard working? Their first lessons should come from what they see at home and from family members, whether they live near or far.

"Data shows we need to help our kids have a sense of community. Because we move more and are not as connected (to extended family) as previous generations, parents need to help build that sense of community. Family meals are a place where it can be practiced on a regular basis," Lindsay continued. "That's not to say that having a family meal every night will solve the world's problems. But it will help ground our kids."

One of those surveys was conducted by Lifeway Research. Study coauthor Scott McConnell said his survey results were similar to those of the CASAColumbia poll regardless of whether people called themselves churched or unchurched.

"We live in a very experience-based society, and sometimes we overlook the God-given experience of just eating," McConnell said. "We forget we can make dinner a time to spend with people we love, good food, and good conversation—anyone would consider that a good time. It's almost a perk of being in a family."

And the perk of having dinner together is that parents can truly start finding out what's happening in their children's lives.

"Any time you ask your kids questions and ask them to share what happened in their day you're showing love," McConnell observed. "Obviously, it's a great time to make that kind of investment, to pause and to pray when everyone's ready to dig in. There's something more important than your hunger. We're acknowledging the God who is providing for us. It doesn't take long to acknowledge God, and it's an important lesson. The conversation that follows really is an investment in one another and your family."

Therapist DeAnne Kinsey said that many families who want to reconnect first have to disconnect from the distractions. Too many activities? Too many work hours? Too much technology? Get out your day planner and cancel a few of the things that are keeping you from your home and your family, Kinsey recommended.

"In therapy, we determine that some families or couples do not spend *any* quality time together and the prospect of carving out time can be overwhelming. I might recommend that they start with very small increments of time—ten or fifteen minutes and then build up from there."

In fact, she added, it is the overscheduling that leads to stress, which leads to family dysfunction. When families start having dinners together, start with ground rules if early efforts feel more like "misses" than "hits." Kinsey said parents and children should agree on boundaries about what will be discussed and the level of respect that will be afforded to one another. "Parents who make the effort are showing their children how much they value them, teaching where priorities should fall and nurturing positive communication and many other invaluable skills," she said.

❧

While this book focuses on familiar names and faces, there are ordinary people with extraordinary stories of family bonding, too, including Paul Houghtaling. When he talks about things that are most important to him, he talks about two key decisions he's made: The first was to become a Christian; the second, to propose to Anne Clarke, the woman who is now his wife. Of course, he's made many decisions about his life and future, but this kind and thoughtful young man keys in on these as the most valuable.

Why? Because these are the two that his parents told him would be the most significant decisions of his life. Raised in a Christian family, Paul was one of those kids who paid plenty of attention to advice from his parents and other significant adults in his life. Dinners were always eaten as a family, and they always began with prayer. His father, an airline pilot, wasn't always home on Sundays, but when he was, that family meal together was a special occasion.

"We were a sit-down-and-eat-at-the-table family, whether Dad was in town or not," said Paul, a native Texan and medical resident. "We held hands and said our prayers and then we talked about our day and what went on. Looking back—of course, at the time I didn't realize it—it taught us socialization. During the day we could be kids, but at the table we had to have manners. We looked one another in the eye when we talked. Afterward, we all helped clean up."

If his father had been out of town for a while, he'd use dinner conversation to catch up with what had gone on in his absence. "We'd try to give a brief report and it was never enough. We'd have to expand on it," Paul said of himself and his two sisters. "He wanted to know what was going on at school and with friends. This wasn't small talk; it was definitely a time where we were a captive audience to each other."

Among the values Paul has taken from his parents' example was to have a good work ethic and to someday be a good husband and father. "My dad's big message was that you can do whatever you want. You have a brain that works fine, and a body that works fine, and there are so many people who are less fortunate. My mom's was more the 'you're loved' message: that God loves you, and I love you, and that relationships are what matters."

From the time he was seven years old, Paul was a regular at Camp Peniel, a Christian summer church camp at Marble Falls, Texas. Fellowship with other campers and leadership from strong adults helped nurture his spiritual life, he said.

After several years as a camper he got summer jobs there and eventually became a counselor. That's when he met Anne, who'd followed the same schedule: camper, worker, counselor. When they met he was working as a counselor and had his eye on someone else. Anne was working as a lifeguard and had a boyfriend. "It was nice we could start off just as friends. Our first night of really getting to know each other, we sat on my Jeep at this cool lookout point and could see the stars and the city and just talked for seven hours," Paul recalled.

The youths who attended Camp Peniel and worked on staff came from similar backgrounds, so he knew they had similar theological views. He liked that she talked openly about how close she was with her family. She loved the Lord and she loved her family—both were key to Paul. Children may be a few years off, but Paul said he wants to raise them the way he and Anne were raised. "Some people might think we're too close to our families, but we both want to instill that in our kids. We also want to instill a good work ethic and to teach them to stand up for what they believe. It's one thing to say something, but another to go out and do it."

Dinners together involve healthy food and good conversation. They're both big on lingering around the table to talk, whether it's just the two of them or they're entertaining friends or family. Their Sunday dinner traditions are a combination of rituals from both of their families, plus a few new things the young couple bring to the table themselves.

"I don't want to be the family that turns on the TV and zones out at night. Breakfast is quick and lunch is on the go, but I want dinner to be a time set aside when we catch up," he said.

Mary and Bill Burns were raised in small but close-knit families, so it wasn't a surprise when they married and had two children of their own, that life in their household would play out much as it had earlier in their lives.

Bill Burns was an eighth-grade science teacher and his wife was a soft-spoken, beautiful woman with a gift for making every person she met feel that she cared deeply about them. I grew up practically around the corner from the Burns family, and their daughter, DeAnne, was one of my best friends. We met at Christ United Methodist Church in our hometown of Lafayette, Indiana, when we were just four or five years old and my mother was our Sunday school teacher. We were in the same high school sorority and were roommates at Purdue University for a while. When DeAnne was married in that same church, I was her maid of honor, and several years later she, of course, was mine. During high school I spent a good deal of time in the Burns home, gabbing with DeAnne in her room, watching TV and trying to trick her younger brother into making popcorn for us.

Plenty of casual meals were eaten at their kitchen table and they were all good, the conversation always fun. But the meals eaten in the family's formal dining room were special. For Sunday dinner, Mary Burns got out the good china and silver and set a beautiful table. Every dish on the table was wonderful, warm, and comforting. Some dishes were prepared just as her mother had taught her. Others were recipes she collected and perfected herself.

"My strongest memories of our Sunday dinners are from when I was about thirteen and older," DeAnne (Burns) Kinsey said. "My aunt and uncle and cousin were there often. My grandparents were always there. When my other grandma moved up to the area, she was there every weekend, too."

When DeAnne and I went off to college, those Sunday dinners became a respite from pledging and studying, and a quick fix for even the tiniest case of homesickness. When we arrived, we were expected to help set the table or finish up in the kitchen. After dinner, we helped clean up. But in between, well, that's when the magic happened. "I went home almost every Sunday," she said of our college years. "I always brought someone with me and people really wanted to be invited."

One of the stories her family still loves to tell revolves around DeAnne's brother Jeff when he was around ten or twelve years old and Sunday dinner was at their grandmother's house. He loved her chicken and dumplings and wanted to sit next to the big, heavy pot so he'd have quick access to his favorite food. What he didn't realize was that would make him the official "dipper" of the dumplings. For adults it's not a problem, but when you're a hungry ten-year-old boy, it's a tough lesson learned. "I'll never forget that day," said DeAnne, laughing. "He said, 'I'll never sit in the dumpling chair again!' In fact, we still tell that story . . . and we still laugh about it."

The Burns family is a good-natured bunch, but the real source of their humor was family patriarch Bill Burns, who was a great storyteller and a serious practical joker. When he set his sight on you, there was no escape. So DeAnne should have been at least a little worried when she took Jim Kinsey home to meet her parents. They'd met at college at the end of her junior year and went their separate ways for the summer. He spent the summer at Philmont Scout Ranch in New Mexico; she spent her summer at home. They stayed in touch the way college students did in the 1980s—through handwritten letters and the occasional phone call.

When school started up again in the fall, she was expected to take him home for Sunday dinner. "So I took Jim home to meet everyone and we were sitting around the table after we ate. Dad got to talking about an experiment he had to do the next day at school. He called it an antigravity experiment, said he needed to practice, and asked if I'd help."

Bill Burns got a broom, a glass of water, and a chair and led DeAnne into the adjoining living room. Everyone else, still seated at the table, clearly saw what was coming. He stood on the chair, placed the glass of water against the ceiling, and braced it with the end of the broom handle. He asked DeAnne to hold the end of the broom. Then he picked up the chair, returned to the table, and sat down. "I looked over at the dining room table, and everyone was laughing. My mom, my dad, my brother, and my new boyfriend were all laughing. I very quickly realized my fate. The only thing I could do was let the glass fall and get all wet. Then I went into the kitchen, filled it up with more water, and threw it on my dad. That was Jim's welcome to the family."

Of course, neither every day nor every dinner are filled with pranks and laughter. In 1992, DeAnne was five months' pregnant when she suffered a miscarriage. Her daughter, Mary Elizabeth, lived for an hour. It was just a few days before Thanksgiving and she and Jim shifted from the happy glow of impending parenthood to planning a funeral for the little girl they were able to cradle for only a matter of minutes.

"We'd just had the funeral, and we were all really depressed. We debated just skipping Thanksgiving," DeAnne recalled. "Then Mom said, 'We're having Thanksgiving because we still have so much to be thankful for.' So we threw it together at the last minute. It was just immediate family, and it wasn't the big meal we'd usually do, but it was very meaningful. We acknowledged one another and all that we had and all that we had to be thankful for in spite of that overwhelming loss. It is definitely symbolic that our family still sticks together, no matter what."

A more recent setback was the death of Bill Burns after his valiant fight against cancer and its side effects. When DeAnne and her family reflect on his influence they describe their memories of this intelligent and humorous man as "magical."

"Lessons of love and laughter, concern and support, devotion and loyalty will be passed on to all who knew, or even knew of, that legendary dinner table," DeAnne said just months after her father's death. "This gift my parents gave us lives on in my own home. Our table is open to all. On special occasions, we will gather around Mom and Dad's dining room table missing what once was, while enjoying what is and will become."

DeAnne and Jim Kinsey's sons are grown now. Their eldest is a teacher; he and his wife are just starting their own family. Their youngest is just out of college and getting started in life. They grew up visiting grandparents and great-grandparents for Sunday dinners on a regular basis. DeAnne has carried on the traditions of her mother and grandmother and can make an apple pie or any other dish as well as her mother ever did.

What traditions did she take to her own home? "Probably all of them, except I'm certain I never poured a glass of water on my boys when their girlfriends were here!" DeAnne laughed. When her sons are home she likes to make their favorite meals, whether it's a Sunday dinner or special event. Their birthdays are close together and one year they combined their birthday dinners. She told them they could each have whatever they wanted—so they had spaghetti and meatballs and fried chicken with mashed potatoes and gravy. "It was a crazy meal, but the boys didn't think it was odd at all." No, nothing odd at all: just close family, great food, and good times.

❦

Paul and Anne Houghtaling are a couple just beginning to turn their families' traditions into their own. DeAnne and Jim Kinsey are a generation ahead and handing their own traditions down to their sons. Lois Bushong has another story: She has built a "modern family" model of close friends she's made throughout her very interesting life.

The daughter of evangelical missionaries, Lois's earliest memories are of a childhood spent in rural Honduras in Central America through World Gospel Missions. The Bushong family—Lois's parents, she, and her two younger brothers—lived in a small village in the 1950s. Later they moved to Tegucigalpa. But they always were among the Honduran people, learning and living the local traditions. Their friends were Hondurans, and Lois and her brothers grew up bilingual.

At noon, the family ate American-style food and said grace in English. For the evening meal, they ate the local diet—rice and beans, plantains and tortillas, along with seasonal produce and meat—and prayed in Spanish.

Excitement came on Sundays, when her father traveled through jungles to reach the villages where he would preach. "As I think about our traditions, those first years in the small town were very different. At that point, no one had vehicles," said Lois. "I remember my dad riding a mule out to the villages to preach. One of us would go with him and we would ride double in the saddle, Dad in back and one of us in front. Sometimes we'd fall asleep coming back, and the mule just knew the way home."

Later, her parents got a Jeep and the whole family would venture out to convert the poorest Hondurans living in primitive homes in the most rural of areas. When the Sunday sermon was done, the grateful villagers always invited the preacher and his family into their homes. They had little, but they always had enough to share. "The people were very, very poor and for them to offer us food was a sacrifice," she recalled. "Their fixing dinner was their way of saying, 'What we have is yours.' It was pure hospitality and friendship, and it meant a lot. It's very humbling to be the recipient of something like that."

But Lois and her brothers loved the life there—and they loved the food, too. To this day, when she thinks of home cooking, she thinks of black beans and rice, homemade corn tortillas, and plantains. "When people in the United States talk about comfort food, they say they love meat loaf or macaroni and cheese," she laughed. "When I think of comfort food, I think of refried beans."

Lois and her brothers returned to the States to attend high school and college, but all three returned to their parents' work in one form or another. As a missionary herself, Lois worked with kids and kids' clubs; she trained teachers and youth workers to do the same. She wrote school curriculum in Spanish and translated from English to Spanish. Later, she earned another degree in counseling and now works as a marriage and family therapist in Indianapolis. Her volunteer work is spent helping families—missionaries or otherwise—preparing to travel to foreign countries to live.

When she invites friends into her home now, she passes on the lessons she learned as a child from some of the most impoverished people in Central America: She prepares the dishes from her childhood that evoke the strongest emotion she knows—love. "Feeding people is my way of showing them that I care about them. It's a special time together, and nothing means more to me than to share what I have with you," Lois explained.

℘

Whether shared by a young couple just getting started in life, a family with teenaged children, or someone later in life, Sunday dinners are a special event. When you ask anyone—East or West Coast residents, Midwesterners or Southerners—about their family dinner traditions, their eyes light up. The meals may have regional or cultural differences, but the sentiment is the same: good food, good conversation, good times.

Some family dinners are utilitarian, both prepared and eaten quickly so adults can dash off to work or meetings or children can be shuttled to sports practices or games—or so either can get on with homework or household chores. But those are weekday dinners.

Sunday is special. People sleep in a little, drink an extra cup of coffee, and linger over the newspaper before heading off to worship. Once a family returns home, the day—or a big part of it—is often spent together. Extended family may drop in. "Like family" friends are invited over. Together they carry on decades-old traditions and create new memories. This day of rest that prepares us physically for the week ahead also comforts us spiritually. When we gather around the table to drink in the scents of favorite foods, we bow our heads to thank God for our blessings in what may be the perfect intersection of faith and family.

This chapter has introduced you to several ordinary people who've had extraordinary experiences in their lives. The rest of this book brings more familiar names to you: pastors of megachurches or preachers who've won special places in our hearts.

Houston, Texas, is known for its many megachurches, including the nation's largest, Lakewood Church, where Joel and Victoria Osteen are co-pastors. In the same city you'll find the country's largest Southern Baptist church—Second Baptist, lead by Rev. Dr. Ed Young—and the country's largest United Methodist church, Windsor Village, lead by Rev. Kirbyjon Caldwell and his wife, Pastor Suzette Caldwell. All three families are featured in the chapters that follow, along with pastors from San Antonio and Dallas, Texas; Sacramento and Los Angeles, California; suburban Nashville, Tennessee; Denver, Colorado; Queens, New York; Greenville, South Carolina; and the University of Notre Dame in South Bend, Indiana. The pastors are from many different denominations or have found their calling at nondenominational churches.

My hope is to give you a peek into the lives—and dinner tables—of these well-known pastors. They may live their lives on a national stage, but you'll find that in many ways they're not that different from the rest of us. They have victories and setbacks. They welcome people into their lives and occasionally have to say good-bye. They live their faith and raise their families in a way that is at the same time effortless and intentional in a very busy world. Try their favorite dishes. Borrow a few of their family traditions. Take the best from them and make more memories for your own family.

CHAPTER TWO

Bishop T. D. and Serita

Jakes

{ The Potter's House ❦ Dallas, Texas }

Thank You for the food we are about to receive
for the nourishment of our bodies.
In Christ's name, amen.

WHEN DADDY COOKS, THE HOUSE IS FULL

Serita Jamison was a young woman with a big crush. She lived in a small West Virginia town and had recently graduated from college with a degree in drama and mass communication. She was single and active in her church and, somewhere along the way, heard a sermon by a young preacher on the rise, T. D. Jakes.

It was the late 1970s, and the young minister was mostly a guest preacher at Pentecostal churches around Charleston, West Virginia. But Serita occasionally found herself at conferences or church events where he was a speaker or choir director. She liked his message, and she liked his style, too. So much so, in fact, that her friends teased her that she "looked at him like he was a cookie."

The tall, handsome Reverend Jakes, however, had absolutely no idea who she was.

Serita may have been smitten, but she was also too shy to introduce herself and flirt her way into a date. In an effort to get T. D. to notice her, she sent him "secret pal cards," greeting cards with warm messages but no signature. For weeks on end, she regularly sent him these notes, and naturally, T. D. became increasingly curious about the identity of his admirer.

Eventually, Serita decided to reveal herself. In a long letter, she explained who she was, why she admired him, and why she had been sending the notes. While her friends knew about her crush, none knew about the secret pal cards. So imagine everyone's surprise when, not long after T. D. should have received her letter, T. D. was a guest preacher at Serita's church. When she saw him up in the pulpit that day, she was petrified. After the service, a friend took Serita by the arm and marched her up to the pulpit for an introduction.

Serita said she would have protested, but at that point she could barely speak. She knew he would have gotten the letter by then and would recognize her name. What would he say? What should she do?

The introduction was made and Serita stood frozen, lucky that she didn't faint right on the spot. "He smiled and looked at me and said, 'Do you know where a single man can get a home-cooked meal around here?'" Serita recalled. "All I could say was, 'I don't know, but I'll ask my mother.'"

So on that Sunday in West Virginia, Bishop T. D. and Serita (Jamison) Jakes had their first date: It was a Sunday dinner at her mother's home.

It would be easy to say that the couple lived happily ever after, because they have. But that's hardly the ending to their story. The couple married in 1981 after dating for a couple of years. T. D. had opened his own church, the Greater Emmanuel Temple of Faith, and worked full-time at Union Carbide in South Charleston, West Virginia. Serita went from a home in which other people did the cooking to a home in which she was expected to prepare full meals every day and send her new husband to work with a plated lunch, as his mother had.

"When we got married I knew how to make two things, meat loaf and spaghetti, and they were made from the same recipe except that one was runnier than the other," Serita said as her daughters—Sarah Henson and Cora Coleman, both Food Network junkies—rolled their eyes and giggled. "Awhile later, T. D. told me that he hated meat loaf, so I was relieved that I didn't have to make it."

So T. D. taught Serita to cook his favorite dishes and the eager learner caught on quickly. As she gained confidence she expanded her repertoire: fried chicken, creamy mashed potatoes, cabbage rolls with corn bread, and southern-fried apples, among other dishes her children rave about. To this day, her children say that the most soothing thing to eat after being ill is their mom's secret recipe for Cream of Wheat. Before each meal, the family says a prayer. Sometimes it's drawn from what's happening in their lives, but most of the time it's the same simple prayer that T. D.'s father said at mealtime when he was growing up.

"Eating dinner together on Sunday is the most important thing we do. Through it, we are able to keep our family focused and keep our hands on one another," T. D. Jakes said. "My children are apt to come home with McDonald's any other day, but Sunday is sacred."

T. D. speaks nostalgically of his childhood: His father was a janitor who built a cleaning business that at one time employed fifty people. His mother was a teacher who had many talents. He remembers hanging around the kitchen while she cooked, hoping to lick the bowl after she made a pound cake. When T. D. was still a boy, his father suffered renal failure. So T. D. grew up quickly, getting himself to school, helping around the house, and learning to cook.

Early in their marriage, the Jakes were busy growing their church, creating outreach ministries, and raising their children. They hosted Back to the Bible conferences and handled all of the cooking themselves, often cooking for up to 150 people. The two would sit in their kitchen, peeling potatoes and preparing dishes for hours before the events started.

They also ran what amounted to a small catering business to support their young church, by making dinners and selling them to nearby office workers on weekdays.

On Sundays after morning services, it was their church community's tradition that a family from the congregation would invite the pastor and his family—all seven of them—home for dinner. It was an old-fashioned tradition compared with the way many people lived in the 1980s, but that was life in West Virginia.

It's also the way Serita grew up. A coal miner's daughter, she was raised by an aunt and uncle—Everett "Goldie" and Ruth Martin—because her parents worked a lot and couldn't find adequate child care. From the time she could talk until she was seventeen, she called them Mom-mom and Pop-pop. When it was their turn to host their pastor's family for Sunday dinner, they'd get out their best dishes and make special food. "The families would always do their absolute best," said Serita as she looked back on her childhood and life as a young pastor's wife. "They'd often make the gospel bird—chicken—and greens."

Every now and then, Sunday came without an invitation to dinner and the Jakes would have a more laid-back afternoon. Serita would make sandwiches at home and take them to church with her. After services, they'd eat their picnic there, then she'd put the twins—Jamar and Jermaine—down for a nap on pew cushions until congregants returned for the evening service.

In their first ten years at Temple of Faith, Jakes increased his congregation from ten people to one thousand. He started his radio ministry, *The Master's Plan*, and a year later launched his Back to the Bible workshops. Then came a special sermon, "Woman, Thou Art Loosed," which launched a book, television ministry, movie, and, finally, conference that still draws many thousands of women annually. A men's version, "ManPower," came a year or so later to provide a similarly empowering message for moving past pain and poor choices to be productive and grow as adults living Christ's message.

By the mid-1990s, T. D. had become nationally known. An accountant for his church was from the Dallas area and had learned that some prime property—the former Eagle's Nest church operated by evangelist West Virginia Grant—had become available. He urged Jakes to consider a move for his growing ministry. The Jakes and their advisers from the Temple of Faith visited the site and came to the conclusion that God was calling them to Texas. They did their homework, constructing business, public relations, and marketing plans. Then the Jakes moved to Dallas to open the Potter's House. They took with them fifty families from West Virginia who wanted to be a part of this new ministry.

So on a warm spring day in May 1996, Bishop T. D. Jakes took the pulpit for the first time at the Potter's House before 1,500 people. "We invited people, and they came," Serita said.

Each Sunday, it seemed, there were more new faces in the audience. The Potter's House today counts thirty thousand members; some fourteen thousand attend services there weekly. Even more quickly, the day-to-day routine for T. D. and Serita—whose children then ranged in age from Thomas "Dexter" Jr., who was still an infant, to twins Jamar and Jermaine, who were young teens—went from ordinary to, well, something that might be hard for most kids to imagine.

"All we knew was West Virginia, and everything we had left behind," said daughter Cora. "Dad had never been on a large scale like this, and not everybody was happy about it. We lived on the faith that it was God's decision. I believed that everybody would be okay and grew stronger in my faith because of it."

Sarah, who's married to Washington Redskins linebacker Robert Henson—whom she met when both were students at Texas Christian University in Fort Worth—agreed. "Things happened so quickly that we really learned to hang on to one another," she said.

Faith played a role in taking the Jakes family to Dallas and played a role in keeping them tight-knit, said Serita. "Faith is the nucleus," she declared. "That is who we are; it is not just our profession." The kids wore beepers for security purposes. Other children asked them for their autographs. Family meetings weren't just about house rules and vacation plans but were also about business plans and international travel.

Dallas is plenty friendly, but after-church traditions were different. Families no longer invited them home for chicken dinners. At first, the exhausted Jakes family would retreat to a restaurant for dinner and relax before returning to church for the evening service. Their first Christmas in Texas, when Serita and T. D. asked their children what they wanted for gifts, the kids were unanimous: They wanted their parents' time. The family took a two-week vacation to Hawaii. When they tell the story today, the kids still light up with stories from that memorable holiday. "We wanted quality time away from Dallas with our parents," said Cora. "No gifts. Just togetherness."

Never mind that their hotel had great food and a Burger King nearby; Serita Jakes still wanted to feed her family. "There we were in a five-star hotel in Hawaii, and my mom goes out and buys an electric skillet and some chicken, and she was making fried chicken in the hotel room," recalled Sarah. Serita was unruffled: "We wanted chicken."

It wasn't long before the other children in Dallas didn't necessarily see the Jakes kids as celebrities, they saw them as friends. Jermaine, Jamar, Cora, Sarah, and Dexter wanted to eat at home and wanted to bring their church friends home with them. Cora was active in the church's youth ministry and brought friends—sometimes five or six at a time—home for the afternoon. Sarah brought home her share of pals, too. Dexter, now still in high school, usually reports in to his mom before leaving church so she'll know how many extra mouths she'll be feeding. Some Sundays, it's three or four; others, he might take a caravan of ten kids home.

"The house was never empty. We always invited friends and people from church," Sarah remembered.

Sunday afternoon became an important time for the Jakes family: the one day of the week that everyone had nothing but church, one another, and a growing circle of loved ones. T. D. and Serita are the "Bishop" and "First Lady" to adults at the Potter's House, but on Sunday afternoon they answer to "Daddy J" and "Mama J"—or any number of variations on that theme—to the young men and women they greet at church, as well as those who join them at home.

"Sunday dinners are the catalyst to hold grown adults, teenagers, and midlifers together," T. D. said. "We all laugh and joke and deal with issues."

Both T. D. and Serita always wanted to be good parents, but they also want to be good role models, particularly for young people.

"Because of the demographics of our church, there are lots of kids from single-parent families," Sarah noted. "They come here and say that it's like *The Cosby Show*. They can see another version of what a family can be—and it never has anything to do with how much we have, it's about who we are. They see that we have a mom and dad who love each other and have stayed married. We all want to have in our families what we've had growing up."

She wants to be the kind of parent that her mother and father have been for her, she said. "Even though my dad is famous and travels a lot, I have always felt that he thinks I'm special. I can call my dad directly; I don't go through public relations or a secretary. Whether he's about to go onstage to preach or he's about to speak to the president, I can call him and say, 'Dad, I have a problem,' and he will stop everything."

Sarah is now officially a resident of Virginia and Sundays are game days during football season. But she always feeds her husband a home-cooked meal on Saturday nights. She jokes that because she doesn't know how to cook for a small family, they invite neighbors and friends from the team, mostly players who were in the same 2009 draft class as Robert.

In the off season, Sarah and her young family return to the Jakes home in Dallas to live in the guest house. "On Sundays, we sit around the table and go over our childhood stories and try really hard to embarrass one another," joked Sarah as Cora laughed in approval. "We do imitations, especially of Mom's soft, whispering voice. We always joke that if we got in trouble, Mom would give us the whispering of a lifetime."

"We've all moved away, so Sundays are the day we can eat and lie around the house like we have no responsibility," Sarah said as daughter Makenzie enters the room, signing that she wanted something to eat.

Cora proudly bragged that she taught her niece sign language before she was old enough to talk. Quick to respond, Sarah set her straight: "All you did was buy the video."

The sisters, just eleven months apart, finish each other's sentences. When there's an eager audience and stories to be told, the young women respond to every cue. But in a crowd, they're the first to shield each other.

Cora complimented Sarah for the "pasta night" tradition she created so the siblings could gather for each new episode of the prime-time drama *Grey's Anatomy*. "She makes this pasta dish with a cream sauce she makes from scratch. And she makes it with chicken and with shrimp so you can have it either way."

Sarah complimented Cora's Food Network adaptations: pound cake, Krispy Kreme bread pudding, apple turnovers, and peach-glazed ham.

T. D. Jakes travels a good deal for work, but is in Dallas almost every Sunday to deliver his sermon. Then he heads home with his brood to eat, relax, and reconnect. As much as they may like the dishes from any other family member, it seems the head of the household is also the biggest personality in the kitchen.

"My dad loves to go grocery shopping, and he likes to tell people that he can feed an army out of what we have in the refrigerator," said Sarah. "He thinks he should have his own cooking show."

Sarah and Cora spoke teasingly, but in their hearts they were bragging about their father's cooking. Their list of Dad's dishes is long, and he's been making cherry cobbler, white bean chili, and corn bread for so long that he doesn't need a recipe. Whether it's a weeknight or a special Sunday dinner, when T. D. is doing the cooking, Serita calls all of her children to let them know. "When we tell the kids that Daddy's cooking, we have a full house," she said.

T. D. smiled in acknowledgment. He knows that when he cooks it's an event, but he admitted that he loves cooking for a crowd. He gets high compliments for his baked beans, a simple recipe with an untraditional technique. He puts dried pinto beans with chicken broth, ham hocks, carrots, onions, and spices in a covered turkey roasting pan and bakes it overnight at a low temperature. "You cook them overnight, get up in the morning, and there you are," he explained.

But of all the dishes his family loves, what is his personal best? "They say," T. D. replied, pausing for dramatic effect. "They say my banana pudding cannot be beat."

It's his mother's recipe, but he uses a slightly different technique (he heats the milk in the microwave rather than in a double boiler). Will he share the recipe? No way. "I can't tell you because if I did, I'd have to kill you," he laughed.

His mother suffered from Alzheimer's disease in her later years, but when she was lucid they'd talk about family memories, favorite foods, and, of course, banana pudding.

"We always debated whose banana pudding was the best," he recalled, smiling at the memory of his mother. "The last time I made it for her, I asked her if it was as good as hers. She tasted it and looked at me and said, 'Almost.'"

ABOUT THE JAKES FAMILY

THEIR CHURCH: The Potter's House, Dallas, Texas

DENOMINATION: Nondenominational

ATTENDANCE: 14,000 attend weekly services; 30,000 members.

THEIR ROLES: Bishop T. D. Jakes is CEO of the Potter's House and is the author of numerous books, the first of which was turned into a movie, *Woman, Thou Art Loosed*. He is also a poet, playwright, movie producer, and Grammy-winning music producer.

THEIR FAMILY: The Jakes have five children: twins Jamar and Jermaine, Cora, Sarah, and Thomas "Dexter" Jr. They have two grandchildren, Malachi and Makenzie.

COMMUNITY OUTREACH: The church has more than fifty outreach programs, including youth mentoring, home ownership classes, entrepreneurial training, and a charter school. Outreach extends to developing countries such as Kenya, where teams from Potter's House sponsored construction of water wells and a primary school, and Nairobi, where they funded health-care facilities.

ON THE NATIONAL STAGE: The Potter's House holds four major annual conferences: the Pastors' and Leadership Conference; ManPower; MegaFest; and Woman, Thou Art Loosed. Jakes delivered the morning church service before President Barack Obama's 2008 inauguration.

READ MORE: Serita Jakes is the author of *The Princess Within: Restoring the Soul of a Woman*, *The Crossing*, and *Beside Every Good Man: Loving Myself While Standing by Him*. T. D. Jakes is the author of many books, the most recent of which are *Let It Go: Forgive So You Can Be Forgiven*, *Wisdom from T. D. Jakes*, *Reposition Yourself: Living Life Without Limits*, and *Why? Because You Are Anointed*. To learn more about the Jakeses and the Potter's House, go to thepottershouse.org.

Country-Fried Pork Chops

··{ Serves 4 }··

This traditional recipe for fried pork chops will transport you to your grandmother's table. Serita Jakes says her technique is simple enough for any home cook to prepare a hearty entrée.

1 cup vegetable oil, for frying

½ cup all-purpose flour

½ teaspoon seasoned salt

Freshly ground black pepper

4 (¾-inch-thick) pork chops

Heat the oil in a large skillet over medium-high heat.

Combine the flour, seasoned salt, and pepper in a paper or plastic bag. Place the pork chops into the bag, seal tightly, and shake it to coat the meat.

When the oil is hot, shake off the excess flour from the pork chops and place them in the hot oil. (The oil should bubble when you put the meat in it.) Cook on each side for 4 to 5 minutes, or until golden on the outside and the juices run clear.

Home-Style Green Beans

{ Serves 4 to 6 }

This foolproof recipe for green beans can be increased for a larger family. If you want to make it healthier, Serita suggests using smoked turkey or turkey bacon instead of traditional bacon.

¾ pound fresh green beans, cut into 2-inch lengths

1½ cups water

6 bacon strips, cooked and crumbled

1 tablespoon seasoned salt

In a saucepan, combine the beans and water and bring to a boil over medium-high heat. Decrease the heat to medium-low, cover, and simmer for 10 minutes. Add the bacon and seasoned salt and simmer for 10 to 15 minutes longer.

Baking Powder Biscuits

{ Serves 12 }

Serita Jakes likes to substitute butter-flavored vegetable shortening in many recipes, including this family favorite, a dense but tender biscuit.

2 cups all-purpose flour

1 tablespoon baking powder

1 teaspoon salt

¼ cup butter-flavored vegetable shortening

¾ cup milk

Preheat the oven to 450°F and put a rack in the center of the oven. Grease a baking sheet and set aside.

Sift together the flour, baking powder, and salt. Cut in the shortening with a pastry blender until the mixture resembles coarse crumbs. Stir in enough milk to make a soft dough. (You may not need the entire ¾ cup of milk, so add a little at a time.)

Turn out the dough onto a floured board and knead it lightly a few times. Pat or roll the dough to a ½-inch thickness. Cut the rolled dough into biscuits with a floured 2-inch biscuit cutter.

Place the biscuits onto the prepared baking sheet and bake for 12 to 15 minutes, or until lightly browned.

Homemade Banana Pudding

·······························{ Serves 6 to 8 }·······························

Nothing sparks debate in the Jakes family faster than a question about who makes the best banana pudding. This recipe is from Serita and makes a spectacular, pie-like dessert. You can also get creative with the presentation by preparing it in ramekins or rustic, oven-safe bowls.

MERINGUE

3 large egg whites

¼ cup sugar

PUDDING

3 cups vanilla wafers

3 bananas, cut into ¼-inch slices

¼ cup all-purpose flour

1¼ cups sugar

2 cups milk

3 large egg yolks

2 teaspoons butter

2 teaspoons vanilla extract

Preheat the oven to 350°F.

MAKE THE MERINGUE: Using an electric hand mixer or stand mixer, beat the egg whites in a large glass or metal bowl until they are foamy. Then gradually add the sugar, continuing to beat until the whites are stiff. Set aside.

MAKE THE PUDDING: Line the bottom and sides of a 9-inch pie plate with a layer of the vanilla wafers. Top with a layer of the banana slices. Set aside.

In a medium-size saucepan, whisk together the flour and sugar. Stir in 1 cup of the milk and turn on the heat to low.

In a small bowl, beat the egg yolks, and then whisk them into the cooking milk mixture. Add the remaining cup of milk and the butter.

Cook over low heat until the pudding is thickened, stirring frequently with a whisk, about 15 minutes. Remove the pudding from the heat and stir in the vanilla extract.

Pour half of the pudding over the vanilla wafers and bananas while it is still hot. Top the pudding with the remaining vanilla wafers and banana slices. Pour the remaining pudding over the top of the second layer of vanilla wafers and banana slices.

Spread the meringue on top of the banana pudding in the pie pan, making sure to completely cover the pudding layer.

Bake for 15 minutes, just until the meringue is browned. Allow to cool, then chill before serving.

Five-Flavor Pound Cake

························{ Serves 12 }························

Cora (Jakes) Coleman loves to bake and this pound cake is one of her favorite things to make. It's rich and moist and the combination of extract flavors takes it a notch beyond the usual traditional dessert.

CAKE

3 cups all-purpose flour

½ teaspoon baking powder

1 cup milk

1 teaspoon coconut extract

1 teaspoon lemon extract

1 teaspoon rum-flavored extract

1 teaspoon butter-flavored extract

1 teaspoon vanilla extract

1 cup (2 sticks) butter, at room temperature

½ cup shortening

3 cups sugar

5 large eggs, beaten

GLAZE

½ cup sugar

¼ cup water

½ teaspoon coconut extract

½ teaspoon rum-flavored extract

½ teaspoon butter-flavored extract

½ teaspoon lemon extract

½ teaspoon vanilla extract

Preheat the oven to 325°F and place a rack in the center of the oven. Grease and flour a 10-inch tube pan and set it aside.

MAKE THE CAKE: In a small bowl, combine the flour and baking powder; set aside. In a measuring cup, combine the milk and extracts; set aside.

In a large mixing bowl, cream the butter, shortening, and sugar until the mixture is light and fluffy. Add the eggs and beat until smooth.

Beat in the flour mixture alternately with the milk mixture, beginning and ending with the flour mixture.

Spoon the cake batter into the prepared pan and bake for 1½ to 1¾ hours, or until the cake tests done. Let the cake cool in the pan on a wire rack for 10 minutes.

Turn the cake out of the pan onto a wire rack. Place waxed paper under the rack to catch any glaze drippings.

MAKE THE GLAZE: In a saucepan, combine the sugar, water, and extracts. Bring the mixture to a boil, stirring until the sugar is dissolved.

Slowly spoon or brush the glaze onto the top of the cake while it's still hot. Let cool completely and serve.

Southern Fried Apples

{ Serves 6 }

Serita has made this side dish for several years and says it goes well with pork, but you can also serve it as part of a breakfast or brunch menu. The syrup produced by the brown sugar and cinnamon perfectly offsets the tartness of the Granny Smith apples.

8 medium-size Granny Smith apples

4 tablespoons (½ stick) butter

½ cup firmly packed brown sugar or Splenda Brown Sugar Blend

½ teaspoon ground cinnamon

⅛ teaspoon grated nutmeg

Quarter and core the apples and then chop them into bite-size pieces.

Melt the butter in a heavy skillet over medium-low heat. Add the brown sugar, cinnamon, and nutmeg and stir. Add the apples and stir gently until they're coated in the brown sugar mixture. Stirring occasionally, sauté for 15 to 20 minutes, or until the apples are tender.

CHAPTER THREE

Pastors Joel and Victoria

Osteen

.... { Lakewood Church ⟨⟩ Houston, Texas } ....

Lord, thank You for this meal that You have provided.
Bless this food to strengthen our bodies.
Bless our families, and help us to be always mindful
of one another as we honor You.
We pray this in Jesus' name, amen.

TRADITIONS: YOURS, MINE, AND OURS

Some families eat to live. Others live to eat.

When Joel Osteen was growing up in Houston, his father was a Pentecostal minister who started Lakewood Church in 1959 in a vacant feed store. His parents, Dodie and John Osteen, were devoted to their children and to God. But dinner? Well, it was simple, eat-to-live fare, prepared with efficiency. Meals were about getting the nutrition they needed, not about developing worldly palates.

Across town, Georgine Iloff was a mother with other ideas about the food she'd feed her children, Victoria and Don, Jr. She believed that meals should be flavorful and rich. Sometimes they came with sauces, sometimes with an international flair. Always, they were prepared with care and love, the way Georgine's mother and grandmother had taught her. The dinner table wasn't just a place for a meal, it was also meant for Victoria and her brother to learn manners and how to engage with adults in conversation.

For both families, meals began with a table blessing, and parents and children were always together to share them.

"My mother gave us a love for different kinds of food," said Victoria Osteen, now co-pastor at the church she and her husband, Joel, have transformed into a nondenominational megachurch attended by more than forty-three thousand people each week and watched on TV by millions more worldwide. "We ate [whole] wheat bread before it was chic. And we always ate fresh vegetables—never out of a can." Victoria joked that she longed to take a peanut butter and jelly sandwich, chips, and a Ding Dong to school for lunch, but her mother wanted her to eat a more proper "hot lunch" served at school.

But Joel grew up in a home where meals were simple; snacks barely existed; and desserts, well, a sweet tooth could be conquered in just a few bites—and then you put your fork down. To this day, that's how Joel Osteen still eats; when he's full, he's done. He doesn't stuff himself, never goes for second helpings, and rarely finishes a dessert.

But Victoria's mother often prepared big, five-course breakfasts on Saturdays, formal sit-down dinners every weeknight, and holidays with thirty or more family members. Their tables were always loaded with Southern comfort foods. Victoria and her brother, Don, Jr., were born in Huntsville, Alabama, where their father, Donald Iloff, Sr., worked on General Electric's Saturn rocket project. Iloff, a mathematician, moved his family to Houston at the start of the 1960s, in the early days of the space race at NASA.

Victoria's parents were deeply spiritual and raised their children to share their beliefs. Together they read and talked about the Bible and attended a nearby Church of Christ. After Sunday morning services, the Iloffs and other families from their church went to a restaurant, usually Romana Cafeteria, part of the Luby's chain.

"My family always ate . . . and we laughed a lot," Victoria said of the dinners they shared, whether they were at home or with friends in restaurants. "We've always been people who sit around a table and talk and eat. The table's a real gathering place. Joel's family is not like that as much. Maybe that's why they're all skinny," she added with a hearty laugh.

It's not that food wasn't important in the Osteen household. It's just that Dodie Osteen and Georgine Iloff were very different kinds of cooks.

"My mom cooked but it wasn't her favorite thing to do," Joel said. "Not that her food wasn't good . . . it was. But we ate much more plain food growing up."

Victoria tells a story about when her mother-in-law became an empty nester, the first thing she did was "declare her kitchen closed."

Victoria and her brother, Don—chief of strategic operations at Lakewood—are just as close as they were growing up. When the two reminisce, they laugh and joke and can't help but finish each other's sentences. Don Iloff starts a story about how the two of them had chores at home. Victoria had to set the table and sweep the kitchen floor; Don washed the dishes.

"Tell her about setting the table," Don urged, laughing.

On cue, Victoria began: "I would go around the table setting it for the four of us, my dad and mom, me and my brother. I'd go 'fork, fork, fork, fork . . . spoon, spoon, spoon, spoon.' And I'd talk the whole time. I'd say, this fork is for the king and this fork is for the queen. This fork is for the princess and this fork is for the palace dog."

And with that, brother and sister roar with laughter. "Don was so good about it," Victoria said. "He wasn't mean to me. He just let me be his little sister."

Don recalled trips to the cafeteria on Sundays back in the 1960s, when dinner at Romana's after church was something of a Texas tradition. The Iloffs would pile into their car and meet other families from their church at the restaurant, building on the friendships they'd made at church. "We had to dress up for church then, and I always wore a tie," Don remembered. "I just thought everyone went to church and then went out to eat. I remember seeing a boy my age in shorts one time, and I couldn't figure out how he could wear shorts to church."

Holidays were special occasions and when Christmas rolled around, Victoria's family traveled to Columbus, Georgia, where her mother grew up. Victoria's grandparents still lived there, as did aunts, uncles, and many cousins.

They'd all stay together on Christmas Eve, and on Christmas morning, her cousins would get out a guitar and they'd all sing gospel songs and Christmas carols. Christmas dinner was full of Southern comfort food, and Victoria still prepares many of the same dishes for holiday dinners today. There's always turkey, of course, plus sweet potatoes, dressing, vegetables and salads, homemade rolls, and desserts. The traditions with which she was raised—food or otherwise—have only grown as Victoria and her family have. Because she cherishes the time she spent with grandparents, aunts, uncles, and cousins, she wants her own children to have their own, similar experiences. And because the Iloffs and Osteens live close by, no one has to drive too far to stay in touch.

Nowadays, Victoria and Joel host holiday meals for combined Iloff-Osteen celebrations. They set up round tables inside their home, or take them outside if the weather's nice. They've got the details of staging a gigantic family dinner down pat. But when Joel was first introduced to an Iloff holiday spread, well, he couldn't believe his eyes.

"The first Thanksgiving Joel spent with me, he was in awe of the food." Victoria laughed. "He said it was the best food he'd ever had in his life."

Some twenty-four years later, Joel Osteen has gotten used to the spread and the hoard of people. "I remember my first holiday with Victoria's family. There was so much food and it was all delicious," recalled Joel, still incredulous all these years later. "They had these sweet potatoes with cinnamon and nuts—it was almost like a dessert."

In fact, that dish was Senator Russell's Sweet Potatoes, a staple in Southern kitchens, especially those in Georgia, the state Richard Russell served in the U.S. Senate for nearly forty years. Nearly every Georgia cook—including Victoria Osteen's mother and grandmother—prepares some variation of this dish. It taps into some of the South's favorite ingredients, sweet potatoes and pecans, and you'll find these sweet potatoes on the menu at the Osteens every year when the holidays roll around.

Victoria said Thanksgiving dinner these days usually means nearly thirty family members, plus invited friends. "Everybody gets excited, and everybody wants to bring something. My mother brings salad. Dodie brings tea. My sister-in-law Lisa brings mashed potatoes because her husband doesn't like sweet potatoes. He's an Iowa boy. So Lisa makes mashed potatoes, and they're great."

In the evening, after the rush of Thanksgiving is over and the first round of leftovers have been eaten, the family walks over to the Galleria area tree lighting where, with thousands of other Houstonians, they watch as the holiday season gets its commercial kickoff.

Christmas dinner is a lot like Thanksgiving, with the same menu and the same crowd. That holiday for Victoria and Joel Osteen begins with their two children, Jonathan and Alexandra. They set up their Christmas tree in the den and usually sleep around the tree on Christmas Eve—a tradition from Victoria's childhood.

When their children were younger they'd hide their gifts and conduct a scavenger hunt with clues leading them from one gift to another. "The note might say, 'Where does Mama put her car keys?' and then the kids run to where the car keys are. Along the way there might be a gift, and some of the clues just lead to another clue," Victoria said. "We're all laughing and carrying on the whole time. If my daughter opens her clue and waits half a second, my son will peek at it and yell out the answer to the clue. He's four years older, so he's quicker."

Holiday dinners are special occasions, of course. It's easier to get everyone together and break out favorite family recipes when those dates roll around. But weekday meals, and regular Sundays, too, are a different story. Kids have activities, Victoria and Joel have obligations at church, and the family travels at least once a month for its Night of Hope events all over the country.

To this day, Victoria cooks more the way her mother did. Her family loves Italian food, especially lasagna and pasta dishes. They eat a lot of chicken and fish. When winter rolls around, Victoria breaks out her soup pot to make tortilla soup, chicken soup, or vegetable soup.

Before meals, Victoria or Joel say grace. Sometimes the kids say the mealtime prayer. "When the kids were really young, Jonathan always prayed the same prayer, asking God to look out for our church family, to protect us and keep us healthy. He used to ask all of that for his 'cousins, relatives, and ancestors.' His prayer didn't deviate a lot and we never corrected him, but we do tease him about it a little now," Victoria said.

Around the table, conversation isn't heavy. They talk about the kids' schooling and friends.

"We put a lot of emphasis on family. Our whole life is our children and Christian values. It's part of our conversation every day," she said. "We spend a lot of time around the table. I'd like to say we have deep philosophical discussions, but we don't. We just enjoy one another."

Joel said that was the way he was raised, too. He and his siblings to this day remember the fun they had together as children. Dinnertime conversation was often lighthearted. Only once did his father try something more serious and spiritual at the dinner table. One night, John Osteen declared to his wife and children that after dinner they were going to have a Bible study. As Joel recalls, the Bible study only lasted about fifteen minutes because he and his siblings got to giggling and weren't too cooperative. They can laugh about it now—every one of them is in a ministry, and they all read the Bible daily. Joel's brother, Paul, is a doctor who has a medical mission in Africa. His sister, Lisa Osteen Comes, preaches at Lakewood and works in administration. Tamara Osteen Graff and her husband pastor at Faith Family Church in nearby Victoria, Texas. Joel's youngest sister, April Simons, and her husband Gary pastor at High Point Church in Dallas.

Lisa Osteen wrote a book in 2012 that explained a little bit of Lakewood's history from her own experience. She was born with a birth defect that should have left her with a severe disability. John and Dodie began a regimen of Bible reading and prayer for their daughter, who eventually overcame that disability. That seemingly unexplainable recovery, she said, influenced the whole focus of their ministry, and they founded Lakewood in 1959 as a place that believed in the miraculous power of prayer.

John and Dodie and their children grew Lakewood to a membership of more than 5,000 in its first twenty years. When John died of a heart attack in 1999, Joel stepped up as senior pastor. Continued growth made it clear they'd need a much bigger sanctuary, and Lakewood opened at its current location on U.S. 59 in Houston in 2005 in a renovated former sports arena—first called "The Summit" and later renamed "Compaq Center"—where the Houston Rockets NBA team played for twenty-eight years and won back-to-back national championship titles in 1994 and 1995. The professional hockey team the Houston Aeros played there, too, as did the former Houston Comets WNBA team, which won its four national championship titles all under this roof.

But today the Osteen family—Houston boosters of a different kind—keep the building busy with services, in both English and Spanish, as well as Bible studies and other faith lifestyle programs.

Lakewood is the center of their own family life, and the couple says they don't have to work hard to convince their kids to make family and church a priority. "We want things to happen naturally so we lead by example," Victoria explained.

From the time her children were young they were involved at church. She wanted Sundays to be a great day, so she made sure there were special treats they otherwise wouldn't get. She'd buy doughnuts for breakfast, and later in the day they got Coke—neither is something you'll find in the Osteen home very often.

"I wanted the kids to think Sunday was always a good day, a fun day," she said. "They're with family, and they're with friends. I haven't had to force or teach that, it's the way we live."

Jonathan plays guitar in a band that performs on Sunday nights. Alexandra gets to see cousins and friends. When the kids were younger, it wasn't unusual for their cousins to spend the afternoon with them.

Joel Osteen worked at his father's church in television production. Today he still wants to handle the editing of tapes from church for the service that gets televised around the world. And it's not unusual for media interviews to be scheduled on Sundays after church, so some days he may not get home from church until five p.m., he said. Thousands of Houstonians flock to Lakewood for services, but the church is also the city's biggest tourist attraction, drawing visitors from across the country and around the world. Its services can be seen in one hundred countries, broadcast primarily on the Trinity Broadcasting Network and Daystar Television Network.

Victoria and Joel are pretty much in sync with each other on everything—everything, that is, except sweets. "Joel will always save room for sweets," said Victoria. "He doesn't eat a lot of sweets, but he'll eat some."

He loves a chocolate cake she makes; there's almost always one in the house. Whereas she'll serve herself a slice and eat it all, Joel eats only enough to be satisfied—even if it's just a few bites. "He chooses restaurants by their desserts," she laughed. "He likes to go to La Griglia for its chocolate mousse cake."

Victoria said that she tries to keep her sweet tooth under control, but it's tough. "Every day I say, 'Today is the day I'm going to quit eating sweets.'"

Regardless of whether a meal is eaten out or at home, the Osteens share them with one another. Faith and family pair naturally and easily in their lives. "We don't have to talk about faith and family at dinner—we just show it," said Joel. "If you're all together you can't help but have fun."

ABOUT THE OSTEEN FAMILY

THEIR CHURCH: Lakewood Church, Houston, Texas

DENOMINATION: Nondenominational

ATTENDANCE: 43,000 attend weekly services.

THEIR ROLES: Joel Osteen is pastor and Victoria Osteen is co-pastor.

THEIR FAMILY: The Osteens have two children: son Jonathan and daughter Alexandra.

COMMUNITY OUTREACH: Lakewood partners with over seventy-five local charities and nonprofit organizations, such as food pantries, financial assistance, prison outreach, shelters, and youth organizations.

ON THE NATIONAL STAGE: Joel Osteen is the most-watched inspirational figure in the United States. His weekly broadcasts are watched by more than 20 million people every month. His show is broadcast to almost one hundred nations worldwide.

READ MORE: His book *Your Best Life* was on the *New York Times* best-seller list for more than two years and sold more than 4 million copies. He is also the author of *I Declare: 31 Promises to Speak over Your Life*. Victoria's message to women is found in her book *Love Your Life*. She also is the author of the children's books *Unexpected Treasures* and *Gifts from the Heart*. To learn more about the Osteens and Lakewood Church, go to lakewood.cc.

Holiday Turkey

{ Serves 18 to 20 }

It may take only four or five hours for a turkey to bake, but Victoria Osteen insists on getting up super early to put the turkey into the oven, because she uses broth from the turkey to make gravy and dressing.

1 (20-pound) turkey
Salt
Freshly ground black pepper

Preheat the oven to 350°F.

If you're using a frozen turkey, allow it to thaw completely in the refrigerator. (This could take four to five days for an 18- to 20-pound bird.) Rinse the turkey well and remove the neck and giblets from inside the turkey.

Sprinkle the turkey with salt and pepper and lay it in a roasting pan, breast side down. Add 20 ounces or more of water to the pan (so you'll have plenty of juice to use in other dishes).

Cover the roasting pan with a lid or foil and bake 4½ to 5 hours (see Note). Remove the turkey from the oven and pour the broth through a strainer into a large bowl for later use in dressing and/or gravy. Allow the turkey to sit at least 15 minutes, then slice for serving.

{ NOTE }

If your turkey is larger or smaller, adjust the baking time by allowing 15 minutes per pound of turkey. The USDA recommends baking a turkey until its internal temperature reaches 165°F on a meat thermometer.

Senator Russell's Sweet Potatoes

{ Serves 12 }

This might just be the most-baked holiday side dish in the state of Georgia. It's named after Richard Russell, who was governor of the state and, later, a U.S. senator. Victoria Osteen's mother's family is from Georgia and the dish goes way back on their traditional holiday menu. Joel Osteen jokes that at the first Thanksgiving with Victoria's family, he wasn't sure if it was a side dish or a dessert.

POTATOES

10 medium-size sweet
  potatoes

2 large eggs

1 cup granulated sugar

1 teaspoon vanilla extract

¾ cup milk

½ cup (1 stick) butter,
  melted

TOPPING

2 cups firmly packed light
  brown sugar

½ cup all-purpose flour

½ cup (1 stick) butter,
  melted

2 cups chopped pecans

Preheat the oven to 350°F.

MAKE THE POTATOES: Bake the sweet potatoes until soft, 35 to 40 minutes. Allow them to cool enough to be handled, then peel and mash them. Push the potatoes through a ricer or sieve and place in a large bowl.

In a small bowl, mix together the eggs, sugar, vanilla, milk, and butter. Add to the sweet potatoes and mix.

Pour the potato mixture into a 9 by 13-inch baking pan.

MAKE THE TOPPING: Whisk together the brown sugar and flour. Stir in the melted butter until crumbly, then add the pecans. (If the mixture isn't crumbly, add more sugar.)

Sprinkle the topping over the potato mixture and bake for 50 minutes, or until the topping is bubbly.

Corn Bread Dressing

{ Serves 18 to 20 }

Victoria Osteen's dressing recipe combines the holiday's traditional, savory flavors of corn bread and sage. Packaged corn bread mixes can simplify the preparation.

12 cups corn bread, broken into small pieces (see Note)

3 to 4 teaspoons rubbed sage

5 biscuits, crumbled into small pieces

4 large eggs, beaten

½ cup (1 stick) butter

3 cups finely chopped celery

3 cups finely chopped onion

6 cups turkey broth

Preheat the oven to 350°F.

In a large bowl, combine the corn bread pieces, sage, and crumbled biscuits. Add the beaten eggs and mix. Set aside.

In a medium-size saucepan, melt the butter over low heat. Add the celery and onion, and cook until the onion is translucent, about 20 minutes.

Add the onion mixture to the cornbread mixture and mix well. Slowly add the broth and stir until it is thoroughly incorporated. (The mixture will be very moist.)

Transfer the mixture to a 9 by 13-inch pan and bake for 1 hour, or until golden brown.

{ NOTE }

To get 12 cups of corn bread, prepare corn bread mix in three 8-inch square pans, or one 9 by 13-inch pan plus one 8-inch square pan.

Texas Fudge Cake

{ Serves 12 }

This chocolate cake is a staple in the Osteens' kitchen. Victoria says she makes it every week, and they eat small portions of it every day.

CAKE

2 cups all-purpose flour

2 cups sugar

½ cup (1 stick) butter

½ cup vegetable oil

1 cup water

¼ cup unsweetened cocoa powder

½ cup buttermilk

2 large eggs, beaten

1 teaspoon baking soda

1½ teaspoons ground cinnamon

1 teaspoon vanilla extract

½ teaspoon salt

ICING

½ cup (1 stick) butter

¼ cup unsweetened cocoa powder

1 teaspoon vanilla extract

3¾ cups confectioners' sugar

1 cup chopped pecans (optional)

Preheat the oven to 350°F. Spray a 9 by 13-inch pan with nonstick cooking spray.

MAKE THE CAKE: In a large bowl, sift together the flour and sugar. Set aside.

In a medium-size saucepan, combine the butter, oil, water, and cocoa powder and bring the mixture to a boil. Continue to boil for 2 more minutes. Add the chocolate mixture to the flour mixture and blend.

In a separate bowl, mix together the buttermilk, eggs, baking soda, cinnamon, vanilla, and salt. Add the buttermilk mixture to the batter in the large bowl and mix thoroughly.

Pour the batter into the prepared pan and bake for 35 to 40 minutes, or until a toothpick inserted into the middle comes out clean.

MAKE THE ICING: About 5 minutes before the cake is finished baking, start making the icing by melting the butter in a medium-size saucepan. Add the cocoa powder and vanilla and bring to a boil. Remove the chocolate mixture from the heat and stir in (or mix with electric mixer) the confectioners' sugar ½ cup at a time. Stir in the pecans, if using.

Pour the icing over the cake while the cake is still warm. Let cool completely before slicing and serving.

Banana-Berry Cream Pie

{ Makes two 9-inch pies, or 12 to 16 servings }

This pie is bursting with sweet berries and bananas, offset by the round, creamy flavor of whipped topping. It's an Osteen tradition at Thanksgiving and Christmas.

1 (8-ounce) package cream cheese

1 cup sugar

2 envelopes whipped topping mix, such as Dream Whip

2 prebaked 9-inch piecrusts

3 bananas, sliced thinly

1 (21-ounce) can blueberry or cherry pie filling

In a large bowl, cream together the cream cheese and sugar.

In a separate bowl, prepare the whipped topping according to the package instructions.

Fold the whipped topping into the cream cheese mixture until thoroughly combined.

Line the pie shells with the banana slices. Top the banana slices with one-fourth of the can of pie filling per piecrust. Top each pie with whipped topping, then finish with the remaining pie filling.

CHAPTER FOUR

Pastors Samuel and Eva
Rodriguez

·········{ New Season Christian Worship Center and Cantico Nuevo }·········
Elk Grove, California

Gracious Father, we render unto You thanksgiving as we gather
around this table of faith, family, and fellowship.
At this table we take not for granted the daily bread provided
and ask You to supply the needs of all families according
to Your riches which are in glory. At this table
we remember the poor, hungry, orphan, and widow
and ask for Your daily provision. At this table we acknowledge
Your greatest gift, salvation through Christ.
In Jesus' name we pray, amen.

POLITICS AND RELIGION AT DINNER? YOU BET

When church was over on Sunday mornings, that's when the fun began for Sam Rodriguez. His parents, Samuel and Elizabeth Rodriguez, piled their three children into the car and headed for her parents' home.

"The first thing you would do is smell the food. Even as you were parking you smelled the food," remembered Sam, who with his wife, Eva, pastors the New Season Christian Worship Center and its Spanish-language counterpart, Cantico Nuevo, in the Sacramento, California, suburb of Elk Grove. "You'd hear the voices, and let's just say it was never an introverted gathering. We had loud music, a lot of loud music," Sam laughed.

Sam described his family as very matriarchal—and these dinners were at the home of Andrea and Randolph Nuñez, his maternal grandparents who had twelve children and eighty-six grandchildren. So when Sam Rodriguez—a first-generation Puerto Rican American—talks about the Sunday dinners he and his sisters had growing up in Bethlehem, Pennsylvania, they're nothing like what most people experienced. "I spent Sunday afternoons with an incredible amount of people," he said. "Every Sunday dinner was the proverbial holiday dinner. It revolved around my grandmother and we loved it," he said. "She was a loving granny and a loving mom."

His family's story is one that is distinctly American: an immigrant family that came to the United States with hopes for a better life. His parents worked hard—his father worked for Mack Truck for more than thirty years; his mother was a teacher's assistant. They raised their children to value hard work and education, and they instilled in them the values they learned in Puerto Rico and in the Assembly of God churches where they worshipped.

"When I think about the Hispanic community, it's about *familia*," Sam said. "It's not an exercise of a daily routine, it's who we are. It's critical to our daily activities, at the heart of who we are."

So when Sam talks about his family, he can't help but start the conversation with stories about those noisy megadinners filled with aunts, uncles, and cousins and the life lessons he drew from them. He remembers the kids' wanting their own space, often setting up their tables outside and filling their plates with traditional Caribbean fare after everyone paused to pray. Grace was lead by Sam's grandfather, Randolph Nuñez. After his death, the baton was handed down to the family's leading spiritual figure, Sam's uncle, Randolph Jr.

Samuel is only half joking when he says that the dinnertime prayer was the only time it was quiet at a Sunday dinner. Because once it was over and dishes had been passed, the family enjoyed talking about current events, debating politics and other issues, joking around, and laughing at pranks. "It was an open forum, like Food Network meets *Meet the Press*. Food, politics, church happenings . . . it was very eclectic conversation," he recalled. "The issues of religion and politics, people say you don't talk about them. Not at our table. Lay it out there and see what happens."

Young Sam fine-tuned his debating skills while he devoured plates of roast pork and rice with peas. Sometimes they had *tostones*, which are fried plantains, or *pasteles*, a tamale-like dish using plantains instead of cornmeal and filled with chicken or beef. The dessert table also held an ethnic flair, with flan, coconut, and *arroz con dulce*, a sweet rice pudding. "I don't remember cakes or sweets other than coconut desserts. Cookies and cupcakes weren't there for dessert," he said.

At some point in time, Eva went from being the cute girl at Sunday school to the attractive young woman who accompanied Sam to these dinners. She grew up in Puerto Rico, but had moved with her parents, Raul and Lydia Feliciano, to the United States when she was eleven so that her older sister could get better health care. They, too, lived in Pennsylvania's Lehigh Valley, but her extended family was still in Puerto Rico. She returned there briefly when she was fourteen, but returned to stay when she was fifteen.

With her family, mealtime was a quieter time to meet and talk, to share the events of their day. Holidays were bigger gatherings, when they visited grandparents, aunts, uncles, and cousins, sometimes splitting holidays between her mother's and father's side of the family in Puerto Rico. Her mother was one of five children and her dad was one of four, so those gatherings seemed full of life, with lots of people, food, and joking around.

Sam and Eva first knew each other as friends, but by high school they were dating. College came next, and then the couple married.

"I loved going to holiday dinners with him; there'd be over two hundred people there. It was amazing to see them all there at one house, eating at the same time, the music going and the talking. I remember when his uncle showed up as Santa Claus. It was amazing," Eva said.

Along the way Sam and Eva—who have been married twenty-four years now—had three children, Yvonne, now twenty-two; Nathan, nineteen; and Lauren, sixteen. Early in their marriage, Eva worked as a translator for a school system. Then she was busy raising their children, and Sam worked for the Assemblies of God denomination as an evangelist, district youth director, author, and church planter.

In 2000, the National Hispanic Christian Leadership Conference (NHCLC) recruited Sam to lead the organization, which now represents more than forty thousand Hispanic churches in the United States. It required a move to Sacramento, California, far away from the comfort of family and the Lehigh Valley.

A few years ago, Sam said he spoke at a Bishop T. D. Jakes ManPower Conference and returned to California determined to start a new multiethnic church. "My desire was to see a church that emerged as a community of Christ followers committed to facilitating an atmosphere where every person experiences an authentic encounter with the presence and power of God," he said.

Until then, church work had primarily been Sam's job. But both he and Eva are now ministers through the Assemblies of God church and the couple trades off on pastoral and administrative duties at their churches, with Eva handling sermons at Cantico Nuevo and Sam preaching at New Season. Their ministry began with eighteen people—children included—meeting in a home. Less than two years later, more than one thousand attend Sunday services.

The Rodriguezes' Sunday dinners now are more intimate gatherings with immediate family and occasional friends, but the traditions of home are always evident. When Sam and Eva finish their two Sunday morning services, they head home for family time. Yvonne and Nathan are off at college, but they're home every weekend. "They want time with their family and always go to church with us. It's our community time, our time together." Eva explained. She usually cooks, but even if dinner was premade, or is ordered out, it's still on the table for all to share.

Sam may relish the big gatherings he attended as a child, but he sees great value in a meal shared with just his wife and three children.

"It's when we come together and share concerns in our lives, school, church developments, my travels, or their mother's adventures," he said. "It's *the* time. It's not just eating. It's about the conversation and interaction, jokes, and spirit of the moment."

Around the table, Yvonne, the eldest, is the family philosopher and psychologist. Nathan's sense of humor keeps everyone laughing. And Lauren keeps everyone guessing about which side of any argument she might fall on.

In addition to sharing the highs and lows of their own lives, they're not afraid of tackling any topic. These days, politics gets discussed a lot, either what's happening in the news or the national issues and events in which their father is involved. Through his role at NHCLC, Sam advocates for more humane federal policies, including immigration reform. "Our children have no qualms discussing politics at the dinner table," he said. "After I came back from a meeting at the White House—meeting with President Obama or meeting with Congress—they're very interested in what went on, and I share it with them."

Sam tells his children that they don't have to come home every weekend—if they have other things to do, they're free to spend Sunday elsewhere. "They say, 'absolutely not.' They like to be around their parents. I don't blame them. I'm a very likable fellow," he said, to hearty laughter from Eva.

Perhaps it's more than their father's charm. There is the factor of their mother's cooking. "Eva has to be one of the best cooks on the planet. She truly is," Sam said. "We could go to fancy restaurants, but I prefer Eva's cooking over any other option out there."

"My primary influence is my mother-in-law, Elizabeth. She taught me every traditional Puerto Rican dish I know," Eva stated. "I learned to cook Italian and American dishes by trial and error, then Elizabeth took her time and instructed me on the culinary art of Caribbean cooking."

When Elizabeth Rodriguez planned to make a dish that was one of her son's favorites, she invited her daughter-in-law over for a lesson. Eva would arrive, notebook in hand, and the two women started building what has become a special relationship. "She didn't measure anything, and I had to figure it out and write down the portions," Eva said.

Her family's Puerto Rican heritage is evident in most everything Eva prepares. Such seasonings as adobo and *sofritos* factor into every dish, whether it's traditional Puerto Rican fare or American food—salads, soups, or pasta dishes—she adapts to the style of cooking she knows so well.

"We love rice and peas; I make it at least once a week," said Eva, starting a recitation of the dishes she grew up loving and now prepares for her own family. There's traditional roast pork, which now is more of a special-occasion entrée for the Rodriguez family—and chicken dominates their menu. There are also *tostones*—sometimes sweet, sometimes savory. And London broil with white rice, heavy on sautéed onions and vinegar is another favorite.

When the kids are home, they help out in the kitchen: Yvonne is great at entrées and Lauren likes to make rice. When dinner is over, they help clean up, too. Then they relax in the living room—if it's winter, there's a fire in the fireplace—and get ready for Eva's special coffee, an espresso-like brew. "Coffee is a separate moment," Eva said. "Dinner might be an hour, ninety minutes. Then we leave the kitchen or dining room and gather around the fireplace."

"It's round two," chimed in Sam. "Some people have after-dinner drinks; we have after-dinner Puerto Rican coffee. There's more conversation, and it gets more sophisticated. We have more macro conversations about big-picture items: life decisions; [or] our daughter might talk about her major or graduate school ideas."

Everything goes up a notch or two at Christmas, a special time of year when the Rodriguezes invite friends from the community or the church home for dinner every night during the holiday week. "We make a lot of pork and rice. Our friends aren't used to Puerto Rican food. They come for my famous Puerto Rican dinner," Eva said with pride. "But by the time January comes, we're done with rice for a while."

Sam and Eva Rodriguez are fiercely protective of their family and the time they spend together. And they make every minute of it count, hoping their children, as second-generation Hispanic Americans, can continue to move the conversation forward.

"Our family dinners are a constant affirmation of our core values. I want my children to see transparency, to see what integrity looks like," Sam declared. "Life at home should not differ from life in the pulpit. We want them to see that we are living out the Gospel and not just preaching it."

ABOUT THE RODRIGUEZ FAMILY

THEIR CHURCH: New Season Christian Worship Center and the Spanish-language Cantico Nuevo, Elk Grove, California

DENOMINATION: Assemblies of God

ATTENDANCE: More than 1,000 attend weekly services.

THEIR ROLES: Sam and Eva Rodriguez are both senior pastors at New Season/Cantico Nuevo, Assemblies of God churches.

THEIR FAMILY: The Rodriguezes have three children: daughters Yvonne and Lauren, and son Nathan.

ON THE NATIONAL STAGE: Sam Rodriguez is the president of the National Hispanic Christian Leadership Conference, which serves 15 million Hispanic Christians and has more than 40,000 member churches. He also serves on the board of directors for Gordon Conwell Theological Seminary, the National Association of Evangelicals, and Christianity Today.

READ MORE: Sam Rodriguez is the author of *Path of Miracles*. To learn more about Sam and Eva Rodriguez and New Season Christian Worship Center, go to nhclc.org or newseasoncwcchurch.com.

Pernil (Roast Pork)

{ Serves 6 to 8 }

Adobo and Sazón seasonings lend a Caribbean air to this pork dish that is the centerpiece of their holiday entertaining. Low-and-slow cooking keeps the meat tender and moist.

1 tablespoon adobo seasoning (see Note)

2 teaspoons Sazón seasoning (see Note)

1 teaspoon dried oregano, or 1 tablespoon chopped fresh

1 teaspoon garlic powder, or 1 clove garlic, pressed

1 tablespoon freshly ground black pepper

1 (3-pound) pork shoulder

In a small bowl, mix the adobo and Sazón seasonings with the oregano, garlic, and pepper. Set aside.

Place the pork shoulder in a large roasting pan, and with the fatty side of the pork shoulder facing up, slice horizontally into the side of the roast. Sprinkle the seasoning mixture inside the pork roast, where you created a slit. Cover and refrigerate at least overnight or for up to one day.

Preheat the oven to 350°F. Cover the pan with a lid or aluminum foil tightly sealed around the edge of the pan and bake for 1½ hours. Halfway through the baking time, remove the foil and bake for an additional 1½ hours (see Note).

{ **NOTES** }

If you're using a larger roast, allow 1 hour of cooking time per pound of meat.

You'll find adobo and Sazón seasonings in the ethnic food aisle of your supermarket.

Potato Salad

{ Serves 6 to 8 }

Apples add a sweet twist to Eva Rodriguez's potato salad recipe—another in her long list of "famous for" dishes.

5 potatoes (about 2 pounds)

1 apple, such as Granny Smith, Braeburn, or Gala

3 hard-boiled eggs, chopped

2 tablespoons finely chopped green olives

1 teaspoon salt

½ cup mayonnaise, or more to taste

Paprika, for garnish (optional)

Fill a medium-size saucepan halfway with water and heat it over medium heat until the water begins to simmer.

Peel the potatoes and dice them into ½-inch cubes. Add the potatoes to the water and cook about 20 minutes, or until the potatoes are fork tender. Drain them in a colander and set aside to cool.

Peel, core, and quarter the apple, then chop it into very small pieces. Add the apple pieces, chopped eggs, and olives to the cooled potatoes. Season with salt and gently stir until everything is evenly distributed. Add the mayonnaise and gently stir until the mixture is coated, adjusting the quantity of mayonnaise to suit your taste.

Refrigerate for at least a few hours to let the flavors blend. Sprinkle with paprika (if using) and serve cold.

Arroz con Gandules
(Rice with Pigeon Peas)

{ Serves 10 to 12 }

This traditional Latin rice dish gets its flavor from the *sofrito*, Sazón, and adobo seasonings, which bring aromatic herbs such as cilantro, oregano, and garlic to a base of tomato, peppers, and onion. It is Eva Rodriguez's signature dish.

3 tablespoons corn oil

3 tablespoons *sofrito* seasoning (see Note)

½ cup tomato sauce

2 tablespoons finely chopped green olives

2 teaspoons Sazón seasoning

1 teaspoon adobo seasoning

1 (15-ounce) can green pigeon peas, drained

3½ cups water

3 cups raw long-grain white rice

Salt

Heat the oil and sofrito seasoning in a large pot over medium heat for about 2 minutes. Add the tomato sauce, olives, Sazón seasoning, ½ teaspoon of the adobo seasoning, and the peas, and stir to combine.

Add 3 cups of the water and bring the mixture to a boil. Add the rice, stir, and cover the pan with a lid. Cook until the rice absorbs the water, about 20 minutes.

Reduce the heat to low. Add the remaining ½ teaspoon of adobo seasoning and the remaining ½ cup of water and sprinkle with salt. Cook for about 15 more minutes before serving.

{ NOTE }

Goya makes a good *sofrito* seasoning.

Flan de Queso (Cheese Flan)

This decadent dessert lies somewhere between the custardy texture of a flan and the rich flavor of cheesecake. Try it once and it will rise to the top of your favorite-finishes list.

8 ounces cream cheese, softened and cubed

1 (12-ounce) can evaporated milk

1 (14-ounce) can sweetened condensed milk

5 large eggs

1 teaspoon vanilla extract

1 cup sugar

Preheat the oven to 350°F.

Place the cream cheese, evaporated milk, condensed milk, eggs, and vanilla in a blender and blend until all ingredients are thoroughly combined. Set aside.

Place the sugar in an 8-inch round glass baking dish. Cook the sugar on the stovetop over low heat until it melts and turns a medium golden color, 6 to 8 minutes. Be sure to stir often; don't let it burn.

Pour the cream cheese mixture over the caramelized sugar. Cover the baking dish with aluminum foil and place the dish in a larger baking pan filled halfway with water. Bake for 55 to 60 minutes, or until the center of the flan tests done.

Run a knife blade around the edges of the baked flan and then invert the dish onto a serving platter. Remove the dish from the platter. Allow the flan to cool, then refrigerate until ready to serve.

CHAPTER FIVE

Rev. Mike and Jeannie
Glenn

{ Brentwood Baptist Church ❧ Brentwood, Tennessee }

*Father, we are grateful for this day and all
of its opportunities and challenges.
We are grateful for the love around this table.
We are grateful for our food because it reminds us
of Your care, both seen and unseen.
Use this food to make us strong that we may serve
You without hesitation.
So, at the end of the day, You won't regret
that You gave these hours to us.
Amen.*

DAD, TELL ME THE ONE ABOUT . . .

The story about the strawberry trifle—told properly—takes input from the entire Glenn family.

Jeannie Glenn was anxious for a visit from her brother and sister-in-law, Mark and Kay Powers. Valentine's Day was near, so Jeannie wanted to make his favorite cake, from their mother's recipe.

Mike Glenn still laughs at the incident that happened ten years ago. "She was going all out, making it in these heart-shaped pans she had just bought."

But Jeannie didn't realize that the new pans were shallower than the round cake pans she usually used for baking. So as the batter rose, well, you can imagine what happened.

"It was like the blob in our oven," described Mike, senior pastor at Brentwood Baptist Church in Brentwood, Tennessee, a suburb of Nashville. "It was coming out of the pan and dripping over everything, and it wasn't done in the middle."

Jeannie got out another pan and finished off the uncooked batter in it, wondering what she'd do with the mess. Their twin sons—Craig and Chris, who were teenagers at the time—got in on the action, too, gathering in the kitchen to survey the mess. Craig re-members it as a holiday when aunts and uncles were coming over and they all were more than a little preoccupied with getting the house ready and getting food prepared.

"We got it out of the oven and I thought, 'There's no way this will be like Grandma's cake,'" Craig said. "We made do because we had so many people there, and they were expecting dessert."

Jeannie was beside herself, of course, but her family was supportive. "Just put it in your trifle dish, and we'll put ice cream on it," Mike suggested. "That'll be great."

So that's what they did. They cut up the cake, dropped in some ice cream, drizzled icing on top, and declared it strawberry trifle. "It's one of our jokes now," Mike laughed. "If we see something really messed up, we look at one another and ask, 'Do you think we can make trifle out of that?'"

Later, everyone got a good laugh from the out-of-control cake that turned into a beautiful—and delicious—dessert. The story, everyone agreed, was too good not to tell.

Stories, after all, are what the Glenns are all about. When Craig and his brother, Chris, were growing up, long after dinner was over, they were still in their chairs at the table, listening to their dad talk about life, family, and the lessons he learned along the way.

The Glenns' traditions may have evolved throughout their marriage, but the seeds were planted a generation earlier, as John and Barbara Glenn raised their sons, Mike and Mitch, in Huntsville, Alabama. The elder Glenns were originally from Mississippi, but John Glenn left for a job at Redstone Arsenal in Huntsville. After several years helping produce military goods, John opened a TV and appliance store, which kept the family busy all week long, Mike recalled. He remembers many weeknight dinners of takeout food and after-school free time spent waiting on customers. But when Sunday rolled around, Barbara Glenn rolled out her best recipes, made the comforting dishes for which Southerners are famous, and created memories around the dinner table.

"Sunday dinner was a big dinner for us because we'd all be at home after church. My mother made traditional Southern fare," Mike said, describing the roasts, mashed potatoes, and rich pies and cakes she made, "and Daddy told stories." As a boy, Mike saw his father as a great jokester and storyteller; he could hold court in any crowd for his ability to get every punch line just right. Many of John Glenn's stories came from his childhood in a Mississippi farm family he loved to describe as "so poor we thought dirt was a toy."

"You don't know it at the time, but you come to understand that those stories are who you are," said Mike. "They tell you how God has worked across generations in your family. You learn from those stories how to respond to challenges when they come to you."

Mike studied speech and drama at Samford University in Birmingham and then headed to the Southern Baptist Theological Seminary in Louisville. There he made many friends, including Mark Powers, who was also a seminarian. Mark mentioned to Mike one day that his sister would be visiting and asked if he'd like to join them for lunch. Mike smelled a setup and hightailed it out of the conversation quickly.

Mark and his sister, Jeannie, grew up in Columbia, South Carolina, and were members of a Baptist church there until Jeannie heard about a dynamic preacher, Rev. Ed Young, who was getting a lot of attention at First Baptist in Columbia. (Young later left the Carolinas for Houston, where he turned the city's Second Baptist Church into the largest Baptist church in the country.) When Jeannie switched churches, her family followed.

That night, Mike and a friend went to see the movie *The Lion in Winter* and discovered that Mark, his wife, Kay, and a beautiful blonde were sitting in the row right behind them. "Mark said, 'This is my sister,' and I said, "My word,'" Mike recalled. "He asked me about lunch again, and I told him I've had some slack in my schedule, and I think I'll be able to make it." In the blink of an eye, Cupid had shot Mike Glenn straight through the heart. Mike joined the Powers family the next day at church and then for lunch. He invited Jeannie out for pizza that night and something clicked. "Three months later we were engaged, and ten months later we were married," Mike said. "It was love at first sight for me, but I don't know how long it took her."

Jeannie said she "was a little slow to catch on," but she knew there was something special between them, and they maintained a long-distance relationship for a while. "At some point over the next months, before we were engaged, I heard him preach, and that's when it all came together: his personality, his storytelling, and his unique way of presenting what we both believed in, the values in both of our lives. It sealed everything for me. I never thought I'd marry a minister, but I did."

They shared faith and values, but there were differences in the way their families spent time together. While Mike grew up without extended family nearby, he still felt connected to them through his father's energetic storytelling. Jeannie, on the other hand, had all of her relatives on both sides of her family in her hometown. She had sit-down dinners with her parents and two brothers on weeknights. On Sundays after church, they gathered either at her parents' home with extended family or they went to her grandparents' home.

"I particularly liked going to my mother's mom's house. Together they prepared a huge meal with three meats and sides and two to three desserts. I think she had to skip Sunday school in order to do that," Jeannie said. "She'd go to an early service and rush home to get the last of the meal together. I think she cooked most of Saturday, too."

If they gathered at her parents' home, the meals weren't quite as elaborate, but they were still great. Jeannie said her mom, Wildred Powers, is an excellent cook and most known for her baking skills. Over the years, her mother won many awards at county and state fairs for her cookies, cakes, and pies.

After Jeannie and Mike married in 1980, they settled into family life in South Carolina, with Mike pastoring churches in Edgefield and Mauldin. Their twin sons—Chris and Craig—came along in 1984. The family moved to Tennessee in 1991, when Mike took the pastor's job at Brentwood Baptist. At the time, the church was considered healthy with nine hundred members. Today, though, more than eight thousand people count themselves among Glenn's congregation.

Jeannie's mother had taught her the basics of cooking when she was younger, then compiled her favorite recipes into a cookbook for Jeannie when she got married. Because Wildred Powers is a champion baker, she taught Jeannie to make the same cookies and pies that she loves to make. From there, Jeannie has found some recipes of her own to adapt, including a cheesecake that her husband and sons love.

Mike's family likes traditional desserts, particularly at holidays. One year at Thanksgiving, Jeannie made pumpkin mousse with homemade whipped cream instead of the usual pumpkin pie. "They looked at it like, 'Where's the pie?'" she said.

But you won't hear Mike complaining about anything Jeannie prepares; his list of favorite foods is long. His favorite meal, lasagna and cheesecake, is one he wants for his birthday each year.

Mike doesn't expect his wife to do all of the cooking. In fact, in recent years he's learned his way around the kitchen and across the grill. He describes his wife's cooking as making dishes "that require patience and planning, including special trips to the grocery store." He, however, cooks from the refrigerator. "I look in and say, 'I can grill that. Let's go,'" Mike said. "I'm a good cook. I can cook anything."

The boys are both married now and Mike and Jeannie Glenn are enjoying a more relaxed family dinner tradition. They've gotten past the picky-eater stage and the busyness of school and activities. Now when their sons and daughters-in-law come over, it's to spend quality time with the people they love the most. "For a while, we lost the tradition because the boys were so busy, and we were so busy. Now we're finding it again with intentionality when they come over on Sunday evenings," Mike noted. "More often than not, we find, that's when family happens."

Jeannie agrees. And in the absence of extended family, they've created their own traditions. "We discovered, and our families discovered, that what's important is being together, laughing and sharing. When there's a holiday, it's whenever you create it," she said.

Both Chris and Craig say they value every minute they've spent around a dinner table with their family, whether it's at their parents' Brentwood home or at their grandparents' lake house on the Tennessee River outside Scottsboro, Alabama. Conversation always starts with topics of the day and what's happening in their lives. But then it shifts to the main attraction: stories.

"Dad is good at telling stories, and he got it from his dad," Chris said. "Nothing is more important than sitting at the dinner table with my family, because it's storytime. We laugh a lot at very funny stories told years ago and told all of the time. They're still the same funny stories because we know the people—and sometime it's about us."

"That goes on well until after we're eating," he continued. "We have done that ever since I was young, especially when my grandparents are there or extended family is there. It's more than dinner . . . it's family time."

Craig agreed, adding that, "When we were growing up my dad had always had this big sense of family, carried on from my grandparents. It was important to him that we come together at night for dinner and talk about our day. It leads us to a tradition of sitting down at the table."

While the family dynamic is organic, there's intentionality there, too. Jeannie and Mike Glenn brought their sons into the world with every intention of raising them into good Christian men. For Jeannie, that meant drawing on her own childhood. "Through our family dinners I felt a stability and steadiness and, I guess, dependability, that my parents were there and I could count on them," she said. "They gave me a sense, like with my faith in God, in knowing that I had a kind and Christian father role model. You learn to accept more readily that you have a father in heaven. That sounds like a real churchy thing to say, and I don't mean to sound scripted, but I really do think . . . I wanted that for my family."

When Jeannie learned she was pregnant with twins, she and Mike knew that from then on, their world would revolve around their children. Looking back, they agree with Mike's assessment: "No one has had more fun being parents than Jeannie and I did."

The couple describes their sons this way: Chris is the old soul, born one minute before his brother; Craig is the prankster who lives to torment Chris; together, they live to torment their mother, setting up practical jokes just to see if she'll fall for them, Mike said. "The common game they play is how outrageous a story they can tell before she realizes they're making it up," Mike laughed. "They'll pull it a little further, and she'll say, 'Ya'll are making this up.'"

For her part, Jeannie was a good sport. She wanted mealtime to be fun and interesting: "Because I was aware that there were so many preachers' kids who felt pressure to have learning moments through *everything*, our mealtime was just fun and loud and a lot of laughter."

A separate game—for Mike and Jeannie—was seeing what they could get their picky-eater sons to put on a plate. "I had tall and skinny boys, and I was happy if I could get them to eat anything," she said. "But I learned, being a cardiac care nurse, to substitute lower-fat ingredients. I substitute turkey for ground beef in chili, and I use butter less.

I substitute Egg Beaters for regular eggs in muffins or whatever. The boys always loved muffins, and I made those a lot when they were younger."

Sometimes she had to keep the alterations to herself, though. "If they knew about the substitutions, they'd say, 'I'm not eating that, it's got turkey in it,'" Jeannie said.

Just as Wildred Powers taught Jeannie to cook, Jeannie was interested in teaching her sons about food. Craig ended up being a good student, and he talks more about the experience than the end results. "Mom and I used to make breakfast at night, egg sandwiches or waffles, and we made brownies probably once a week. That was a special thing we had," said Craig. "There was nothing special about the brownie recipe itself, just the time we spent together."

The Glenn family also enjoys a special Easter tradition, hosted by Eddie and Saralu Lunn, a couple the family became friends with after moving to the Nashville area.

Jeannie said the couple loves to entertain and about twenty years ago starting inviting friends whose families lived elsewhere for Easter dinner. "Saralu makes a turkey and Ed slices it. We all bring sides and desserts. It reminds me of the way things were when I was growing up," said Jeannie. "My boys love it."

Craig and Chris both describe the Lunns as feeling like extended family. "Their kids are at least five or six years older than my brother and me, but I remember hanging out with them and going to football games," Craig said. "Eddie Lunn taught us how to drive stick shifts in his old Mustang. We always wanted to do something with him."

When the boys were younger, they went on Easter egg hunts in the Lunns' yard. Once they were older, they brought girlfriends to the holiday event and helped hide the candy for the younger children. "It was just something that was too special to miss," Craig recalled. "Their family is our family for sure."

Now that Craig and Chris are grown and married, their relationship with their father and other male role models has changed, they both concede. They learned many things from both of their parents, but at the heart of it all was how to be unique individuals while also being in a close-knit family. "Once I got in high school and college and had the freedom to make my own decisions, my dad became my adviser and confidant," Chris said. "He wouldn't tell me how to approach something but would help lead me into a decision. I gained a huge amount of respect for him then."

Chris said that if there was something he wanted to do he'd write out a plan and take it to his dad. Mike would ask questions, make suggestions and send him on his way. "He'd be proud of me and respect my decision. That was the biggest thing for me," explained Chris. "We really did watch him."

"We're twins, and I'd think that if he gave Craig something, then I should get it, too. But he knows our personalities are like night and day, so how he handles a situation with Craig is different than the way he'd handle it with me. He has made me feel like I wasn't always attached to Craig," Chris continued.

For the past three or four years Mike, Chris, and Craig Glenn have carved out time for each other on Saturday mornings at a Brentwood restaurant, the Puffy Muffin. They sit at the same table and see a lot of the same faces every week. They talk about their wives and their marriages, their jobs, and their faith. Sometimes sports teams enter the picture, but mostly, their time is devoted to whatever is on the mind of the three men at the table.

The tradition began because of football, actually. They're huge University of Alabama football fans and there was a big game on. They had such a good time that when they left the restaurant, one of them said, "Same time, same place next week?" and the others agreed.

"We'll take a secular issue and talk about our Christian perspective. Dad brings things he's preaching on or books that he's read, and we each have topics that we ask one another about," said Chris. "It started out, 'Let's just meet for breakfast and have a good time,' and then it got more serious and became a growth opportunity. We all have mutual respect, we're very curious about new information and are constantly asking questions. It's a brainstorming session where we talk about life, and marriage is a big part of that. We're guys learning how to be better men, and we're our own board of directors."

Whether it's breakfast or dinner, Saturday morning, Sunday night, or any other day of the week, meals are welcomed as one of the most treasured events of the day for the Glenn family.

Craig Glenn said that when he and wife Nan have children, they'll certainly find time to continue the tradition. "Our parents taught us that was an integral part of life. Today a lot of families don't do that, he observed. "Just being able to come together once or twice a week would have a significant impact on a child's life. It certainly did on mine."

When Chris Glenn thinks about the universal urge to sit together and share food and conversation, he thinks of Jesus' journey. "I think it's kind of a natural flow out of how we were taught to study the Bible. When you look at Jesus' life, there's always a part where He comes back and has a meal with His disciples or people He's reaching out to," Chris said. "That's the way we were raised, and I have no doubt it's from my granddad's and my dad's Bible knowledge. It's a big part of our life and we treasure it as a family. The Bible is the foundation of our times together as a family."

ABOUT THE GLENN FAMILY

THEIR CHURCH: Brentwood Baptist Church, Brentwood, Tennessee

DENOMINATION: Southern Baptist Convention

ATTENDANCE: Brentwood Baptist has more than 8,000 members and some 5,000 attend weekly services.

THEIR ROLES: Mike Glenn is senior pastor; Jeannie Glenn is a nurse for the Vanderbilt Medical Center.

THEIR FAMILY: The Glenns have twin sons: Chris (wife Debbie) and Craig (wife Nan).

COMMUNITY OUTREACH: Brentwood Baptist supports mission work, both for evangelism and for service work, around the globe. Hundreds of church members each year participate in Mission Journeys, from disaster relief in nearby states to Haiti, China, Africa, and Europe. Service work ranges from home building and repair to medical and dental clinics, to soccer camps and Vacation Bible Schools.

ON THE NATIONAL STAGE: Mike Glenn is a frequent speaker to seminarians, pastors, and worship leaders.

READ MORE: Mike Glenn is the author of *And God Said . . . YES!* and *In Real Time: Authentic Young Adult Ministry As It Happens*. To learn more about the Glenns and Brentwood Baptist, go to mikeglennonline.com or brentwoodbaptist.com.

Lasagna

{ Serves 10 to 12 }

There was a time Jeannie Glenn tried to use low-fat ingredients to make rich dishes such as this lasagna a little healthier. Now she just makes it with all of the richness of the original recipe, but considers it a treat for special occasions, such as her husband's birthday.

16 ounces uncooked
    lasagna noodles

MEAT FILLING

3 pounds ground chuck

1 pound Italian sausage

1 medium-size yellow
    onion, chopped

1 clove garlic, minced

1 to 2 teaspoons chopped
    fresh parsley

1 to 2 teaspoons chopped
    fresh oregano

Salt

Freshly ground black
    pepper

3 (26-ounce) jars
    spaghetti sauce

1 (12-ounce) can tomato
    paste

CHEESE FILLING

3 large eggs, beaten

24 ounces ricotta cheese

16 ounces small-curd
    cottage cheese

Salt and freshly ground
    black pepper

4 cups shredded
    mozzarella cheese

½ cup finely grated
    Parmesan cheese

1 cup water

Cook the lasagna noodles according to package instructions. Drain and set aside.

MAKE THE MEAT FILLING: In a large skillet, brown the ground chuck and sausage with the onion, garlic, parsley, oregano, and some salt and pepper. Drain, then add the spaghetti sauce and tomato paste and simmer, stirring occasionally, for 1 to 2 hours.

MAKE THE CHEESE FILLING: In a large bowl, whisk together the eggs, ricotta cheese, cottage cheese, and some salt and pepper. Set aside.

Preheat the oven to 375°F and place a rack in the center.

Spray a 9 by 13-inch pan with nonstick cooking spray, then spread some meat filling in a thick layer across the bottom of the pan. Top with a layer of noodles, then a layer of cheese filling, then 1 cup of mozzarella, followed by a layer of meat filling. Repeat the layers, starting with noodles, until all of the noodles, cheese filling, meat filling, and mozzarella are used, finishing with 1 cup of mozzarella and the ½ cup of Parmesan.

Drizzle the 1 cup of water around the edge of the pan and cover tightly with foil. Bake for 30 minutes. Remove the foil and bake for an additional 15 to 20 minutes, or until the cheese on top is golden brown and bubbling. Allow to stand for 15 minutes before serving.

Potato Corn Chowder

{ Serves 8 }

This rich and chunky chowder is a favorite of the Glenn family. Jeannie says she got this recipe from her friend Karla Worley.

6 large potatoes, peeled and cubed

½ cup (1 stick) butter

1 medium-size yellow onion, chopped

1 (4.5-ounce) can chopped green chiles

1 (3-ounce) jar roasted red peppers

24 ounces frozen corn

1 quart half–and-half

1 (14-ounce) can chicken broth

Salt

Freshly ground black pepper

Grated cheddar cheese, for topping

Chopped green onions or chives, for topping

Bacon bits, for topping

In a large soup pot, cover the potatoes with water. Bring to a boil and cook until they begin to get tender, about 15 minutes.

In a small skillet over low heat, melt the butter and sauté the onion until translucent, about 5 minutes.

Drain the potatoes, leaving a little of the water in the pan for flavor. Add the onion, chiles, red peppers, corn, and half-and-half. Add the chicken broth a little at a time, until the soup reaches a chunky but not thick consistency. Add salt and pepper to taste. Simmer for 15 minutes.

Serve in bowls and top with the cheese, green onions, and bacon bits.

{ NOTE }

This soup is good with shredded chicken or crabmeat. If you add crab, also add a tablespoon of cooking sherry to the soup.

You can make this in a slow cooker, omitting the need to cook the potatoes separately. Just put everything—including all of the broth—in the slow cooker on the LOW setting for 4 hours.

Homemade Pimiento Cheese

{ Makes 1½ cups cheese }

This appetizer recipe from Jeannie Glenn's mother, Wildred Powers, is simple but immensely satisfying.

8 ounces shredded or grated sharp Cheddar cheese

1 (2-ounce) jar pimiento pieces

¼ cup mayonnaise

⅛ teaspoon prepared mustard

1 to 2 tablespoons sugar

Crackers, celery, or bread, for serving

In a medium-size bowl, combine the cheese and pimiento pieces. Stir in the mayonnaise a little at a time; don't let it get too soupy. Add the mustard and sugar to taste and mix well. Refrigerate at least 1 hour before serving.

Serve with crackers or celery, or on slices of bread as a sandwich.

Cheesy Bean Dip

····················{ Serves 10 to 12 }····················

Sons Chris and Craig Glenn both love Jeannie's Tex-Mex food, especially this flavorful and cheesy dip. Jeannie credits her friend Betsy Painter for introducing it to her family.

1¼ cups grated Cheddar cheese

1½ cups grated Monterey Jack cheese

1 (8-ounce) package cream cheese, softened

1 (8-ounce) container sour cream

1 (10-ounce) container jalapeño bean dip

1 tablespoon chili seasoning mix

5 drops Tabasco sauce

2 teaspoons chopped fresh parsley

¼ cup taco sauce

Tortilla chips, for serving

Preheat the oven to 325°F. Grease an 8- or 9-inch baking dish.

In a small bowl, stir together ½ cup of the Cheddar cheese and ¾ cup of the Monterey Jack cheese. Set aside.

In a large bowl, blend together the cream cheese and sour cream. Add the bean dip and mix well. Add the remaining ingredients, except the reserved cheeses and tortilla chips, and mix well.

Pour the mixture into the prepared baking dish and top with the reserved cheeses. Bake for 15 to 20 minutes. Serve hot with tortilla chips.

{ NOTE }

This dip freezes well after baking.

Crab Appetizer

{ Serves 12 }

This recipe was given to Jeannie Glenn by a friend in Charleston, South Carolina, where hot crab dip and appetizers are something of a signature snack. You can also premake, and even freeze, the crab mixture before using it.

½ cup (1 stick) butter, softened

1 (5-ounce) jar Old English cheese spread, softened

1½ tablespoons mayonnaise

½ teaspoon garlic salt

½ teaspoon seasoned salt

1 cup chopped crabmeat

6 English muffins, halved

Preheat the oven to broil.

In a medium-size bowl, combine all the ingredients, except the crabmeat and English muffins. Carefully fold in the crabmeat.

Spread the mixture onto the halved English muffins, then cut each muffin half into four wedges. Place the wedges on a baking sheet and broil until the muffins are toasted and the topping is melted and bubbly, about 2 minutes.

Strawberry Cake

{ Serves 12 }

Many Southerners grew up with strawberry cake as a special Sunday treat, and Mike and Jeannie Glenn did, too. This is Jeannie's adaptation of recipes from her mother and mother-in-law and would be a hit on any Sunday dinner menu.

CAKE

1 (18.25-ounce) box yellow cake mix

4 large eggs

¾ cup vegetable oil

1 (3-ounce) package strawberry-flavored gelatin

½ cup frozen strawberries, thawed

½ cup water

FROSTING

½ cup frozen strawberries

½ cup (1 stick) margarine or butter

3¾ cups confectioners' sugar

Preheat the oven to 350°F. Spray two 8-inch round cake pans with nonstick cooking spray.

MAKE THE CAKE: In a large bowl, mix all of the cake ingredients until combined. Divide the batter between the cake pans and bake for 25 to 30 minutes, until a toothpick inserted into the center of the cake comes out clean. Set on wire racks to cool.

MAKE THE FROSTING: Put the strawberries in a small, microwave-safe bowl and microwave briefly to thaw. Drain off the juice from the berries and brush the juice over each layer of cake.

In a large bowl, using an electric mixer on low speed, combine the margarine with the confectioners' sugar. Increase the mixer speed to medium and beat until the frosting is light and fluffy. Add the strawberries and continue mixing until the strawberries are completely incorporated and the frosting is pink.

Invert one cake layer onto a cake plate. Spread ¾ cup of frosting onto the top of the cake. Invert the second layer of cake onto another plate, then transfer it to the top of the frosted bottom layer of the cake. Cover the top and sides of the cake with the remaining frosting. Cut into twelve slices and serve.

Sour Cream Cheesecake

{ Serves 12 }

This cheesecake recipe was given to Jeannie Glenn by her mother and has been adapted to her family's tastes over the years. Treat cheesecake batter gently, as overmixing or overbaking can cause its surface to crack or split.

CRUST

2 cups graham cracker crumbs

1 teaspoon ground cinnamon

⅓ cup sifted confectioners' sugar

½ cup butter, melted

FILLING

3 (8-ounce) packages cream cheese, softened

1 cup sugar

1 cup sour cream

5 large egg yolks

1½ teaspoons vanilla extract

½ teaspoon almond extract

½ teaspoon freshly squeezed lemon juice

4 large egg whites

TOPPING

1 (16-ounce) container sour cream

1 cup sugar

1½ teaspoons vanilla extract

½ teaspoon almond extract

½ teaspoon freshly squeezed lemon juice

Preheat the oven to 350°F. Spray a 10-inch springform pan with nonstick cooking spray.

MAKE THE CRUST: Combine the graham cracker crumbs, cinnamon, and sugar in a medium-size bowl. Drizzle with the melted butter and stir until the dry ingredients are moistened and crumbly. Press the graham cracker crumb mixture into the bottom of the prepared pan. Place it in the freezer to chill while mixing the cake filling.

MAKE THE FILLING: Combine the cream cheese, sour cream, and sugar in a large bowl, and beat with an electric mixer on medium speed. Add the egg yolks one at a time and mix until completely incorporated. Add the vanilla and almond extracts and lemon juice and mix thoroughly.

In a separate bowl, beat the egg whites until stiff. Gently fold the egg whites into the cream cheese mixture just until incorporated.

Pour the filling into the chilled crust and bake for 35 to 40 minutes. Remove from the oven and increase the oven temperature to 425°F.

MAKE THE TOPPING: Mix all the ingredients in a large bowl until combined. Spoon the topping onto the cheesecake. Bake for 10 minutes to create a glaze. Allow to cool, then refrigerate for 6 to 12 hours before serving.

Apple Crunch Mix

{ Serves 12 }

This easy-to-make snack mix tastes like a deconstructed cookie: full of fruit, nuts, raisins, and crunchy cereal, all drizzled in a caramel-like topping. Jeannie Glenn thanks her sister-in-law, Kay Powers, for the recipe.

1 cup crunchy dried apple chips, any flavor

1 cup chopped walnuts

3 cups Quaker Oatmeal Squares cereal, any flavor

1 cup raisins

6 tablespoons butter

½ cup firmly packed light brown sugar

1 teaspoon ground cinnamon

In a very large bowl, combine the apple chips, walnuts, cereal, and raisins.

In a medium-size saucepot, melt the butter. Add the brown sugar and cinnamon and cook, stirring constantly, until the sugar is dissolved. (The mixture should not come to a boil.)

Drizzle the sugar mixture over the cereal mixture, stirring gently as you drizzle, until the sugar mixture is evenly distributed.

Pour the coated cereal mixture onto two baking sheets and allow to cool and dry. Break the snack mix into small chunks. Store leftovers in an airtight container.

CHAPTER SIX

Rev. Martin Lam

Nguyen, CSC

{ University of Notre Dame ✤ South Bend, Indiana }

Good and gracious God,
May Your blessings be upon us and upon the food
we are about to receive. All good things
come from Your blessed generosity.
Through Christ, our Lord, amen.

IN AMERICA, HE FOUND A BROTHERHOOD AND A FAMILY

Rev. Martin Lam Nguyen, CSC, unfolded a delicate silk cloth to reveal the most treasured work of art he has created. It is a book, *Nui Cho* (Mountain Waits), an autobiographical work that combines three thousand images with phrases to tell the story of forty years of his life.

His face is somber; his voice, soft. He strokes the pages of handmade parchment with his fingertips as if conjuring the words, in English and his native Vietnamese, to life.

"Looting."

"Trouble."

"The Funeral."

"The Dead Nun."

Some entries are single words, others are phrases. Each represents a different day or experience from some of the most difficult years of his life—including during and after the Vietnam War when he was a teenager and a young seminarian.

"The Funeral" documents an emotional farewell to a young Vietnamese officer who died in the fierce battle at Mo Duc. The fallen soldier was the older brother of one of Martin's classmates, and he remembers the service and burial as if they happened yesterday.

"Number 495, 'The Forced Joining of Youth Group,'" Martin said, pausing to tell the story. He's fifty-four now, but back then, Martin was a teenaged seminary student in Vietnam when the Communists approached the seminarians, pressing them to be role models for other young adults in the city. "They said we were exemplary youths, and they wanted us to be in the Ho Chi Minh Youth Association," he explained, shaking his head in dismay. "I knew it was a setup so I told them that I couldn't do anything without permission from my superiors. We couldn't be in the group because it would mean we had to renounce our faith. When word got out that the Communists were harassing the seminarians, well, Mass was crowded on Sunday."

Then Martin retrieved another set of pages. These weren't bound like the book, but lay loose in a shallow drawer in a cabinet in his art studio tucked into a small woods at the University of Notre Dame in South Bend, Indiana. Each page had rows of painted images, actually pictures of mountains drawn and then painted in miniature, black and jagged with a sense of mystery and longing. Each of the three thousand text entries matches up with an image from the rows of mountains.

They were the last thing this Holy Cross priest saw as he, his father, and about fifty others fled their homeland in the middle of the night, hoping to be rescued—and freed—once they reached the Pacific Ocean. "I look back and imagine escaping Vietnam into the sea," he said. "All I saw at the time were mountains. The farther we drifted out to sea, the smaller the mountains got. The mountains were like a God, passive but looming larger. I use it as the image of Providence."

"Sometimes we wish God could be more active and visible, directing our path," Martin added. "That's why I use the verb *waits* to portray the relationship. Waiting, for me, acknowledges that."

Martin virtually grew up in the seminary in Da Nang. He was the oldest of six children, and his parents, Duong and Uy Nguyen, sent him there to be educated when he was just ten or eleven years old because it was considered the best school in the area. His family had been Catholic for several generations and two of his aunts were nuns. Religion was important to the Nguyen family, and religious life at the seminary felt natural to young Martin.

As the war intensified, the seminary proved a safe place for him to be, as well. But when the South Vietnamese capital, Saigon, fell to the Communists on April 30, 1975—a day Martin still calls "Black April"—the Nguyen family was torn apart. "The city fell overnight; you couldn't move. It was complete chaos," Martin said.

On that day, his mother fled to safety with the five younger children, but Martin and his father became separated from them and were trapped in the now Communist country. "I was sixteen years old, and we had to live in the moment, day to day. You couldn't plan for the next day. Your survival instinct kicked in," he said of that difficult time. "There are things we are destined to go through without a plan or strength."

Three years later, the International Red Cross managed to get a letter to relatives of the Nguyen family in Vietnam to tell them that Duong and her five children had made it out alive and were in the Philippines. Until then, Martin and his father were tormented by fears of what might have happened. They didn't know whether the rest of their family made it to safety or died trying to escape, shot in the street or drowned in the sea.

Martin and his father had accepted their fate, believing that their own escape was just too risky and that they simply would have to live under the brutal conditions of Communist rule. People were killed for no apparent reason; there was so little food, they literally were starving. But the letter from Duong Nguyen brought hope. Later, she and the children left the Philippines and made it to America. They lived in Pennsylvania and Ohio before finally settling in Portland, Oregon.

A year later, after two other premature attempts, Martin and Uy Nguyen huddled with others in one of two small, wooden boats that set out into Ha Long Bay in the Gulf of Tonkin. "Back then Vietnam wasn't like North Korea, but it wasn't far from it," Martin said. "It was more like East Germany; they would shoot you if they caught you trying to escape."

They were far from the only people to undertake such a dangerous mission. Some three million Vietnamese "boat people" are believed to have escaped the country in the years after the fall of Saigon. It's believed at least five hundred thousand perished trying.

Martin and his father were in Hong Kong for a short time and eventually made it to Portland. Martin spoke good English—the nuns had taught him English and French at the convent—which helped him adapt to life here. By then he was twenty and ready for college. As a Catholic seminarian he enrolled at the University of Portland, run by the Congregation of Holy Cross. Then came the University of Notre Dame, where he earned a master of divinity degree, followed by more art-driven education at Yale and a master of fine arts degree from the University of California at Berkeley.

"It wasn't hard to adjust to life in America," Martin said. "I identified with the Catholic Church and was immigrating to a Christian nation. I was already in that system, so mentally I felt fairly at home."

After his ordination in 1989, he served in a Los Angeles parish for three years. He started teaching painting and drawing at Notre Dame in 1995, after arriving in South Bend, Indiana, full of energy and ideas. He reached out to the city's Vietnamese community and hosted masses on campus, inviting priests from all over to lead them.

Life on the Notre Dame campus and among the Holy Cross Brothers has brought a sense of family to Nguyen. He has been the adviser for the Vietnamese Students Association (VSA) for several years and more recently became the chaplain to Notre Dame's graduate students. He said that the university accepts about twenty Vietnamese American students each fall, so there are usually eighty or more undergraduates who are first-generation Vietnamese Americans. About half of those get involved in the VSA.

For more than a decade, he's regularly lead the students in a Sunday Mass and then gathered them for a communal meal. A few years ago, they asked Martin whether they could celebrate Mass in Vietnamese instead of English. "I thought they couldn't handle

Mass in Vietnamese so I always did it in English. I figured they didn't know enough Vietnamese to do a decent Mass," he said. "But they can get everything on the Internet. They prepared texts and assigned people to do readings. I'm surprised at how well they can speak it and understand it. There's one girl who speaks Vietnamese so well. I close my eyes and listen, and I think this is a girl who is from Hanoi, but, in fact, she is from Minnesota," he added with a hearty laugh.

As somber as he is in talking about his life in Vietnam, he is completely happy and animated describing the pastoral role he plays in the lives of the Vietnamese students for whom he serves as a cultural and spiritual guide.

Many of the teens are away from home for the first time, and while the Notre Dame campus is small and nurturing, it remains a time and place for them to find their own identity. Instead of rebelling to be more independent, his students embrace the ritual and tradition of their roots. They worship in their parents'—and Martin's—native language and dine with him not because they have to, but because they choose to.

"Life is more complex and, in a way, richer than any linear projection that we understand or assume," he said. "What we learn at a young age stays with us and, in a beautiful way, becomes our identity and how we reflect on ourselves and reach out to others."

Martin is proud that he eats lunch with forty to fifty young people regularly. After Mass, they gather for a shared meal. When Martin cooks, he prepares simple food such as chicken and rice. Even if he buys pizzas, he'll still make a salad.

But when the students take charge, they're out to impress. They call home to get their mothers' recipes. They make steaming pots of soup such as *pho*, soft spring rolls (*goi cuon*), or other Vietnamese comfort foods. For a recent meal, a young woman made *thit kho*, a complicated, stewlike entrée of pork and boiled eggs. Her parents own a restaurant in Minneapolis, so she'd called her mother and painstakingly gone over the ingredients and preparation instructions. She knew that the dish was traditional and special and wanted to share it with her friends at Notre Dame.

Once the food is ready, Martin leads them in prayer. Then they all dig in—to eat and talk. "Our conversations are pretty inclusive, covering vast topics about anything they are doing: their home life, food, projects for spring break or summer," Martin explained. "We talk about their families, their studies, food, events at Notre Dame, even a little bit about sports."

Martin remembers the days when he would cook for his fellow seminarians. They were forced to do hard, manual labor in the fields and there was very little food—rice, a few sweet potatoes; on a good day they'd get a little fish. But Martin liked to cook for them, to feed them both physically and spiritually.

So, when he sits down to a table loaded with food on a Sunday at Notre Dame, he works to impart two things to his students: gratitude and sacrifice. "The most important thing I try to relate to these young people is a sense of gratitude. We have a lot of immigrant groups coming to our country, but for the Vietnamese, the conflict is still very fresh in our mind and in our daily life," he said. "We can almost, almost travel freely back to that land."

All it takes is a new book about the Vietnam War, a movie, or a documentary and Martin is transported back to the 1960s and '70s, when freedom was a fleeting hope. He urges his students to understand the sacrifices their parents made to come to America, to learn English and job skills, and raise their children in ways that embrace the best of the Eastern and Western worlds.

"I think that, compared to other Asian immigrant groups, the Vietnamese were poorly prepared for this new life in America. We didn't come here with cash or capital or a profession," he said. "The way people leave China, the Philippines, South Korea, Hong Kong, they are well equipped to make a new life. But a lot of Vietnamese are absolutely unprepared. Ironically, paradoxically, that kind of situation—being unprepared—helped us to appreciate more and deepens our sense of Providence. It frees us from solely thinking of living in a material way and continues to recognize a way of caring and being accepted."

His acceptance extends beyond his student associations. He's the only Vietnamese priest in the Holy Cross order but feels completely at home among his distinctly American religious brothers. On campus, they dine together at Corby Hall. Their cooking staff prepares breakfast, lunch, and dinner, and the men drop in and out of their dining hall as their schedules allow. But none of the priests want to miss—or even be late for—their special Sunday evening get-togethers. They meet for prayers, break for wine and hors d'oeuvres, and then sit down to share a special meal—often a steak dinner—with up to seventy men packed into the small room. When dinner is over, Martin and some of his closest friends among the Holy Cross Brothers walk to a just-off-campus coffee shop to share a hot drink and talk some more.

Most priests on faculty or staff at Notre Dame live in regular dorms with students and wouldn't have any kind of kitchen to prepare food. For several years, that's how Martin lived, but he longed to cook for his friends so that he could share his love for food with them.

So when he could, he headed to his art studio, put away his art supplies, and prepared his favorite foods with electric skillets and hot plates. He propped open the side door so a fan could draw the fumes outdoors. A small herb garden, with rosemary, lemongrass, chives, and mint thrives outside this studio, and he draws on these fresh flavors to season his dishes.

"I am comfortable sharing my cooking, an Asian meal, with a non-Asian friend or students. It's a blessing, a great blessing," he said. "I assume we will have a great time eating the food. When I gather with people, food is another medium to communicate."

ABOUT REV. MARTIN LAM NGUYEN, CSC

HIS RELIGIOUS ORDER: Congregation of Holy Cross, University of Notre Dame; South Bend, Indiana

DENOMINATION: Roman Catholic

HIS ROLES: Associate professor of art (painting and drawing), Vietnamese Students Association adviser, and chaplain to Notre Dame's graduate students

NATIVE OF: Vietnam

RAISED IN: Vietnam and Portland, Oregon

READ MORE: Learn more about Martin Nguyen at nd.edu, and his religious order at holycrosscongregation.org.

Goi Cuon
(Fresh Shrimp and Pork Spring Rolls)

{ Makes 12 servings }

Spring rolls—the kind made with fresh ingredients in healthy rice paper wrappers—are a traditional Vietnamese street food. In America they make a tasty appetizer or light lunch. Their Vietnamese name translates to salad (*goi*) roll (*cuon*) so it's no surprise they're often also called "salad rolls." They're usually served with a fish dipping sauce called *nuoc cham*, but many people like them with a spicy peanut sauce—so here are recipes for both.

NUOC CHAM

3 tablespoons Asian fish sauce

3 tablespoons white vinegar

2 tablespoons sugar

½ cup water

2 cloves garlic, chopped finely

1 chile, seeded and chopped

2 tablespoons freshly squeezed lime juice

HOISIN-PEANUT DIPPING SAUCE

1 cup prepared hoisin sauce

¼ cup smooth or creamy peanut butter

1 tablespoon rice vinegar

1 clove garlic, pressed

1 Thai chile, seeded and minced, or ¼ teaspoon red pepper flakes

SPRING ROLLS

3 ounces vermicelli rice noodles

½ pound ground pork

12 (8½-inch) sheets rice paper

18 cooked shrimp, peeled and sliced in half lengthwise

1 cup firmly packed shredded iceberg lettuce

1 bunch fresh cilantro

1 bunch fresh mint sprigs

1 bunch fresh garlic chives

MAKE THE NUOC CHAM: Combine the fish sauce, vinegar, sugar, and water in a saucepan over medium heat. Stir well and cook until it just starts to boil, then allow the sauce to cool. Stir in the garlic, chile, and lime juice. Refrigerate until ready to serve.

MAKE THE HOISIN-PEANUT DIPPING SAUCE: Place all the ingredients in a blender and blend until smooth. If it's too thick, add warm water 1 teaspoon at a time until it reaches the desired consistency. Refrigerate until ready to serve.

MAKE THE SPRING ROLLS: Start by cooking the vermicelli noodles according to the package directions. Rinse and drain, then set aside.

In a small pan, cook the ground pork over medium heat, using a spatula to crumble it as it cooks so it will be in small pieces. When it's done, transfer the meat to a plate lined with paper towels to drain. Set aside to cool until you're ready to assemble the spring rolls.

To assemble the rolls, fill a large bowl with warm water and dip one whole sheet of rice paper in the water until it softens, then lay the rice paper flat on a plate. In the left third of the rice paper, place three pieces of shrimp in a line, vertically. On top of the shrimp, stack the pork, lettuce, cilantro, mint, garlic chives, and noodles.

To form the roll, first fold the top and bottom toward the center over the filling, then roll the side with the fillings to the right to form a tight roll.

You can serve these immediately or refrigerate for up to 2 hours and then serve with the dipping sauces.

Bo Luc Lac
(Vietnamese Shaking Beef)

·······{ Serves 4 }·······

The Vietnamese name for this dish—*bo luc lac*—translates literally to "shaking beef" because it's tossed in a marinade and then shaken while it cooks in a superhot wok. The marinades for this widely popular dish vary from simple lime-and-seasoning combinations to spicier sauces with soy and chili paste. Served with white sticky rice and a sour-salty-sweet vinaigrette, this dish is perfect for days when you don't feel like spending much time in the kitchen.

MARINADE WITH BEEF

2 tablespoons oyster sauce

1 tablespoon hot water

1 teaspoon sesame oil

1 Thai chile, seeded and chopped, or ½ teaspoon red pepper flakes

1 teaspoon sugar

1 pound beef sirloin, cut into thin slices

VINAIGRETTE WITH ONIONS

½ cup rice vinegar

1 tablespoon superfine sugar

½ teaspoon salt

1 small red onion, sliced thinly

1 tablespoon vegetable oil

1 clove garlic, chopped finely

3½ tablespoons butter

Pinch of salt

Freshly ground black pepper

Cooked jasmine rice or salad greens, for serving

MAKE THE MARINADE WITH BEEF: In a mixing bowl, combine the oyster sauce, hot water, sesame oil, chile, and sugar. Add the beef and marinate for at least 30 minutes.

MAKE THE VINAIGRETTE WITH ONIONS: While the meat is marinating, prepare the vinaigrette by combining the rice vinegar, sugar, and salt in a small bowl. Add the sliced onion, stirring to make sure the onion is covered in vinegar. Refrigerate until serving.

Heat the wok over high heat until very hot. Heat the vegetable oil, then add the marinated beef and cook for about 1 minute on each side. Add the garlic and butter to the wok and cook for 2 additional minutes. Season with salt and freshly ground black pepper.

Top with the vinaigrette mixture and serve with jasmine rice or on a bed of salad greens.

Dau Hu Sot Ca
(Crispy Tofu in Tomatoes)

······················{ Serves 4 to 6 }·······················

If you're looking for a meatless meal to serve your family, this traditional Vietnamese dish combines low-fat tofu with the familiar flavors of garlic, shallots, chiles, and tomatoes. Combined with hot rice, it's a protein-filled meal.

¾ cup vegetable oil

1 (12-ounce) package silken or soft tofu

2 cloves garlic, pressed

1 tablespoon minced shallots

1 Thai chile, sliced finely (see Note)

4 Roma tomatoes, chopped roughly

½ teaspoon salt

2 teaspoons sugar

2 tablespoons Asian fish sauce

½ cup water

6 scallions, cut into 2-inch pieces

1 teaspoon freshly ground black pepper

1 bunch fresh cilantro, for garnishing

Cooked jasmine rice, for serving

Pour the oil into a wok and heat until it's very hot.

While the oil is heating, drain the tofu and then cut it into 1-inch cubes. Add half of the tofu to the oil and deep-fry it until it's crisp. (Cook the tofu in two batches to ensure the oil stays hot.) Remove the tofu from the oil and transfer it to a plate lined with paper towels to drain. Cook and drain the remaining tofu.

Remove the oil from the wok, leaving about 1 tablespoon of oil to use in the tomato sauce. Add the garlic, shallots, and chile to the oil in the wok and cook for 1 minute, or until the ingredients are fragrant. Add the tomatoes, salt, sugar, and fish sauce to the oil and stir. Cook until the tomatoes break down. Add the water to the sauce and bring it to a boil, then reduce the heat to low and simmer for 10 minutes.

Return the cooked tofu to the wok, along with the scallions and black pepper, folding it all together. Simmer for about 1 minute, just to reheat the tofu.

Garnish with cilantro and serve over jasmine rice.

{ NOTE }

If you can't easily find Thai chiles, substitute ¼ teaspoon of red pepper flakes, 1 teaspoon of Thai chili paste, or a small serrano pepper.

CHAPTER SEVEN

Rev. Dr. Ed and Jo Beth

Young

God is great.

God is good.

Let us thank Him for our food.

By His hands we all are fed.

Give us, Lord, our daily bread.

In Jesus' name, amen.

DINNER GETS A HEALTHY MAKEOVER

More than twenty years ago, Jo Beth Young threw out her butter and eggs and declared war on red meat. Her husband had just had a heart-health scare that resulted in a balloon angioplasty procedure, and she decided to have a healthier kitchen.

"I was so determined to cook in the best way for him," said Jo Beth, whose husband, Rev. Dr. H. Edwin Young, is senior pastor at Second Baptist Church in Houston, the largest Baptist church in the country, with more than fifty thousand members, of whom more than twenty-four thousand attend services weekly. "But twenty-five years ago, so many things—the low-fat and low-sodium products—were not available, and you didn't have the labeling that you do now."

Jo Beth had to figure it out on her own, in a time when the Internet hadn't yet taken on a life of its own. When it came time to prepare meals for her family, she substituted Egg Beaters products for eggs, and yogurt for sour cream, learned the difference between saturated and unsaturated fats, and took the salt shaker off the table. "Ed even talked about it in a sermon one time," Jo Beth said with a laugh. "He said, 'My diet is this: If it tastes good, spit it out.' I was proud of my cooking; I wanted it to be good, to be tasty. We are so, in our culture, addicted to salt, sugar, and fat."

Ed made his comment about his heart-healthy diet more than twenty-five years ago, but it hit home again in the spring of 2010 when he felt a tightness in his chest while exercising. Medical tests showed he had significantly blocked arteries, and triple coronary bypass surgery was scheduled.

If Jo Beth's healthy-cooking skills had gotten even remotely rusty, they were sharpened with a renewed interest in good health. "When you look at a recipe you ask, 'Can I substitute canola oil or olive oil? Can I substitute things that are better for you?'" she said. "I never use butter, I use Smart Balance."

Organic products sometimes factor into the mix, as do substitutions for favorite convenience foods. Some of their favorite dishes, such as gumbo, don't make it to the menu often, but when she takes a dish to a potluck dinner at church, she still sticks to her go-to dish, cheese grits—a Southern favorite.

"It's not like when Ed and I were growing up and Sunday dinner cooking," Jo Beth said. "We almost always—literally every Sunday—had roast beef, pot roast with vegetables that cooked while we were at church. Then the leftovers were our Monday night meal. That was the weekly menu. I've heard many people say that, especially people who grew up in the South."

Jo Beth and Ed Young were born during the Great Depression in the same small town, Laurel, Mississippi, where they attended the same school and the same church, First Baptist Church of Laurel. The Depression left no one untouched, so every family, it seemed, had a big vegetable garden and a chicken coop in the backyard.

Ed's father, Homer Young, was an electrician who didn't become a Christian until he was in his forties. At mealtime, his mother would say grace as his father sat silently. Come Sunday morning, Ed and his mother went to church and his dad stayed home.

"When my dad became a Christian, that changed everything. At home, it changed my daddy's language," Ed said with a laugh. "I remember the first time he prayed . . . it was as real as you could get."

Homer Young was hard of hearing, so he didn't go to church often. Instead, he stayed home and listened to a preacher on the radio. But Ed and his mother went to church services every Sunday. "While we were there, my dad made dinner. He usually made fried chicken and mashed potatoes, and he made quite a mess in the kitchen. I remember that because cleaning up the kitchen was my job."

While his pals spent Sunday afternoons at the movies, Ed stayed home to play because his mother was a strict Southern Baptist, and movies were considered sinful. In the evening, he and his mother would return to church.

Life was simpler then. Ed and Jo Beth's mothers were homemakers and school let out at noon so that families could eat a large midday meal—dinner—together. Families spent more time around the table. In some ways, meals were healthier: Vegetables were prepared fresh-picked from the family garden. And in some ways, they were not: Every kitchen had a container full of bacon grease that was used in all kinds of dishes, from corn bread to greens and other vegetables.

Ed said he grew up feeling mostly like an only child—his brother, John Blake Young, is thirteen years younger. But he had two aunts who didn't have children, so it seemed as if he had parents everywhere he went!

Jo Beth grew up with a brother and sister, along with grandparents, aunts, uncles, and cousins galore. Her father had made a big dinner table with a lazy Susan that held the food her mother had prepared. On Sundays, her mother served the traditional pot roast, and when Jo Beth became a busy young mom, she did, too. "My mother was really a good cook. She'd make these little individual pies, putting piecrust on the bottom of a muffin tin to mold the crust, bake them, and then she'd fill them with lemon meringue or coconut cream," she recalled. "All of that does influence you for what you prepare for your family."

Whether they ate a tender pot roast or next-day leftovers, the dinner table was where they were all together. Holidays were spent at her grandparents' home—Jo Beth was the first grandchild in her family—and the adults sat to talk about the events of the day while the cousins played together outdoors. Her grandmother had an organ in her home and sometimes they'd all gather around it and sing.

Conversation at big family events was more formal because her aunts and uncles were educated, professional people and often discussed their work or current events. At home with immediate family, dinner-table discussions were more informal and more personal, Jo Beth said.

Her father, G. B. Landrum, who she described as a God-fearing man with a magnetic personality, left Mississippi to attend Indiana University on a football scholarship, then returned to his hometown even more popular than before. "He was a strong witness for God, and people sought his counsel," Ed said of his father-in-law, who was a longtime announcer at high school football games. "It was almost like you were with the Almighty; he was that welcoming."

Jo Beth agreed. "Daddy, especially, had great ideals and passed those on. Honesty, truthfulness; you knew what he stood for." He lived his faith and shared his values with his children so they would all pass them on to the next generation.

When Ed and Jo Beth started their family, Ed was in the midst of pastoring a succession of small churches—each of which grew substantially under his leadership—in the Carolinas. His first church was in Erwin, North Carolina, where life revolved around the textile mill at which many people were employed.

"We lived in a mill house and could walk to church," Ed said. "Then we moved to Canton, and it was a paper mill town. I'd grow a church, then move and start over again. Every church I'd move to was smaller than the one I'd left."

Those were busy times for the couple, who then had two young sons, Ed and Ben, just two years apart. Son Cliff came along nine years after Ben was born. All three sons ended up in ministry as well. Ed is the senior pastor of Fellowship Church in Grapevine, Texas, a Dallas suburb. Ben is an associate pastor at Second Baptist; Cliff is the lead singer in the Christian contemporary band Caedmon's Call, and also works at Second Baptist.

"When the boys were little, eating out wasn't an option," Jo Beth said. "Ed would preach three or four services, all on Sunday. I'd get the kids ready for church and Sunday school. I would usually put something together the night before so I could cook or bake it the next day or I'd put something in the Crock-Pot or oven to roast while we were at church."

At every family dinner, the Youngs begin by joining hands for prayer. At the end of the prayer, they all raise their hands and shout, "Family!" When the boys were young, dinner conversation revolved around school and sports—all three played high school basketball and Ed's college career began on a basketball scholarship to Florida State University.

"We downplayed that they were a preacher's kids—we'd just say we were a Christian home," said the elder Ed Young of their parenting style. "We never put the preacher's-kid role on our children."

The Youngs moved to Houston in 1978 for the senior pastor's job at Second Baptist. When he first took the pulpit, he'd look out at a congregation of about 350 at any service. Now he ministers to many thousands of members and preaches Saturday nights as well as two services on Sunday mornings. He preaches in person at two campuses and his sermons are broadcast live to three others. And if you don't live in Houston, you can find his sermons broadcast in about any city in the United States.

The move to Houston was hard on their son Ed, the couple said, because he was a senior in high school and his girlfriend—Lisa, now his wife—was still in high school in South Carolina. Ed and Jo Beth remembered the first time their son brought Lisa home for dinner, way back when they were in ninth grade. "One day we asked Lisa to come and eat with us," said Ed. "Our youngest son, Cliff, was probably four then. We gave Lisa iced tea like we drink it in the South. She took one sip and didn't drink any more of it. Cliff piped up and said, 'Mama, Lisa doesn't like your tea.'"

Jo Beth, of course, was a bit mortified, but sweet tea or not, the health-conscious Lisa became her daughter-in-law and the mother of four of the Youngs's ten grandchildren.

Jo Beth Young has always taken pride in her cooking, particularly at holidays. She remembers one Thanksgiving when a grandson with health problems had distracted them from the usual preparations for a large meal. "We were busy, and I thought I wouldn't have time to fix dinner. So I called Cleburne's cafeteria and ordered the meal. You just go on Wednesday and pick it up," Jo Beth said. "The only person I told that I was getting the meal at Cleburne's was Lisa."

This is when Ed piped in to give the story a little more drama: "Jo Beth had never not cooked a Thanksgiving meal."

To add a little ritual to the meal, Jo Beth put a few pieces of candy corn at each place setting on the table and asked all the diners to say something they were thankful for, for each piece of candy corn on their plate. When they got to Lisa, she held up a piece of candy corn and said, "I'm thankful for Cleburne's."

"I said, 'I don't get it,'" recalled Ed, "And Lisa declared, 'We got all the food at Cleburne's.'"

Jo Beth does the cooking in the family, but Ed once decided to try his hand at dilly bread, which he and Cliff liked. Cliff was still pretty young and they decided that together they were going to make the perfect dilly bread. He's not sure they ever truly perfected it, but he declared the experiment good while it lasted.

As their diet has returned to healthier ways, the Youngs have returned to eating many of the fresher whole foods they ate as children—minus the bacon grease, of course.

"His parents always had a garden," said Jo Beth. "They had turnip greens, black-eyed peas, corn, and tomatoes. He thought after leaving home that he would never eat vegetables again, but now those are his favorite things. He'll say, 'I want vegetables,' and he's not talking about green beans, he's talking about peas or greens."

She makes them with chicken broth, which allows her to cut back on salt. She's also a big proponent of fish and likes to roast salmon with herbs and a little olive oil. She roasts vegetables, from okra to cauliflower, zucchini or squash, or even Brussels sprouts. And there's nothing wrong with some convenience foods. For example, she likes to buy tortilla-crusted tilapia at Costco. "It is very good," she said. "Even a child will eat that fish. You bake it in the oven for fifteen minutes, and it's an easy dinner."

Jo Beth believes that parents should teach their children to love healthy food. "I'd rather give my family good food than cookies or things they shouldn't have," she said. "But don't go overboard by not letting them have anything. You need to teach them balance."

ABOUT THE YOUNG FAMILY

THEIR CHURCH: Second Baptist Church, Houston, Texas

DENOMINATION: Southern Baptist Convention

ATTENDANCE: 24,000 attend weekly services; 50,000 members.

THEIR ROLES: Ed Young is senior pastor; Jo Beth Young teaches a Bible study class.

THEIR FAMILY: The Youngs have three sons. Ed (wife Lisa) is founding pastor of Fellowship Church in Grapevine, Texas, and in Miami, Florida; Ben is an associate pastor at Second Baptist; and Cliff (wife Danielle) is lead singer of the Christian contemporary band Caedmon's Call. The Youngs have ten grandchildren.

COMMUNITY OUTREACH: The church is proud of its Second Baptist School, a pre-K through grade 12 college preparatory school founded in 1946. Its graduates include many National Merit Scholars, and its sports teams have won twenty-one state championships in eight sports. They have many other community outreach programs and are known in Houston for their services for Christian singles.

ON THE NATIONAL STAGE: Ed Young was president of the Southern Baptist Convention in 1992 and 1993. His TV ministry, *The Winning Walk*, is televised nationally.

READ MORE: Ed Young is the author of numerous books, including *Total Heart Health* (2005), which he cowrote with his doctors, Michael Duncan and Richard Leachman; *Total Heart Health for Women*, which they cowrote with Jo Beth Young; *The 10 Commandments of Parenting*; and *The 10 Commandments of Marriage*. To learn more about the Youngs and Second Baptist Church, go to second.org or winningwalk.org.

Seafood Gumbo

{ Serves 8 to 10 }

Ed and Jo Beth Young both love soups, especially this gumbo, chock-full of shrimp and crab. And the best part? It tastes even better the second day.

¾ cup canola oil

1 cup all-purpose flour

1¼ cups chopped onion

½ cup chopped green onion

¼ cup chopped celery

1 garlic clove, chopped

1 (8-ounce) can Ro-Tel tomatoes

1 (8-ounce) can tomato sauce

8 ounces frozen sliced okra

2 quarts chicken stock (four to five 14-ounce cans)

1½ pounds peeled and deveined shrimp

½ pound lump crabmeat

¼ cup chopped fresh parsley

1½ teaspoons filé powder

Hot, cooked rice, for serving

Make a roux by heating the canola oil in a large cast-iron skillet. Gradually whisk in the flour and cook, stirring constantly, until the roux is a dark mahogany color, 35 to 40 minutes.

Transfer the roux to a large stockpot over medium heat. Stir in the onion and green onion, celery, garlic, tomatoes, tomato sauce, and okra. Gradually add the chicken stock a cup at a time, stirring as you go. Bring the soup to a boil, lower the heat, and simmer, stirring occasionally, for 3 hours.

Add the shrimp, crabmeat, and parsley and cook a few more minutes. Remove from the heat and stir in the filé powder.

Serve the gumbo over hot, cooked rice.

Cheese Grits

{ Makes 10 to 12 servings }

When Jo Beth Young needs a dish for a potluck at church, this is her go-to recipe. It's rich and creamy and works as the perfect side on many Southern menus.

2 cups raw grits

1 teaspoon salt

½ cup (1 stick) butter

1 pound Velveeta cheese, cut into chunks

1½ teaspoons garlic powder

4 large eggs

⅔ cup milk

Preheat the oven to 350°F. Grease a 9 by 13-inch baking dish.

Cook the grits and salt according to the package directions. Once they have thickened, add the butter, cheese, and garlic powder.

In a small bowl, beat the eggs and milk. Slowly add the milk mixture to the grits, stirring thoroughly after each addition.

Pour the grits mixture into the prepared baking dish and bake for 45 to 60 minutes, until firm. Allow to cool for a few minutes before serving.

Low-Fat Corn Bread

{ Makes 6 servings }

You'll never miss the fat in this corn bread, made richer with the addition of yogurt and creamed corn. It's a great accompaniment to Jo Beth's gumbo.

1 (6-ounce) package corn bread mix

½ cup egg substitute

¼ cup heart-healthy oil, such as canola

⅓ cup canned creamed corn

¾ cup nonfat plain yogurt

Preheat the oven to 425°F. Spray a 10-inch cast-iron skillet with nonstick cooking spray.

Mix all of the ingredients in a medium-size bowl until they are combined but the batter is still a little lumpy. Pour into the skillet and bake for 25 minutes. Slice and serve warm.

Father's Day Pie

{ Makes one 9-inch pie }

When Jo Beth Young didn't think she could get her young children to eat buttermilk pie, she renamed it "Father's Day Pie" for that special occasion. The addition of pecans makes this dessert unforgettable.

½ cup (1 stick) butter

2 cups sugar

2 teaspoons vanilla extract

3 eggs

3 tablespoons all-purpose flour

¼ teaspoon salt

1 cup buttermilk

½ cup chopped pecans

1 unbaked 9-inch deep-dish pie shell

Preheat the oven to 300°F and place a rack in the center.

In a large bowl, cream the butter and sugar until light and fluffy. Blend in the vanilla. Add the eggs, one at a time, beating until each egg is incorporated.

In a small bowl, combine the flour and salt, then add it to the butter mixture a small amount at a time. Add the buttermilk and mix until it's thoroughly incorporated.

Sprinkle the pecans in the bottom of the unbaked piecrust. Pour the custard mixture into the crust and bake for 1½ hours. The pie is done when a knife inserted into the center comes out clean; the filling might still be a little wiggly but should not move around.

Allow to cool, then serve at room temperature. Refrigerate leftovers.

CHAPTER EIGHT

Rev. Randy and Rozanne

Frazee

For food in a world where many walk in hunger.
For faith in a world where many walk in fear.
For friends in a world where many walk alone.
We give You humble thanks, O Lord.
Amen.

DINNER IS FULL OF SURPRISES

Perhaps it was inevitable that Rozanne Bitonti and Randy Frazee would fall in love.

Al Bitonti knew exactly the kind of young men and women he wanted his children to date. So when Rozanne and her brother became teenagers, he moved them from the small Brethren church that had few other teens, to a larger church—Highland Road Baptist—where there was a thriving youth group, which included Randy Frazee, then just a teenager.

"One of my favorite times growing up was Sunday after church, because my dad was there," Rozanne said. "He was an independent grocer and worked long hours, but on Sundays we were all around the table. We'd talk and joke and linger for hours. Sunday is a great time to have a family meal."

Conversation was usually light and spontaneous, and it wasn't unusual for Rozanne and her siblings to bring friends to the table. Mealtime was about having fun and, of course, using good manners. "I wanted my family to know my friends and wanted my friends to know my family. I have great childhood memories," said Rozanne. "For my parents—and I know this now—it was an opportunity for them to get to know who I hung out with."

Back then, her mother, Joan Bitonti, made meatballs on Saturday night so they could have spaghetti after returning home from church on Sundays. Pot roast served as an occasional variation, but the Bitontis were Italian and pasta was a mealtime staple. After Rozanne and Randy started dating, Randy became a fixture around the Bitonti pasta bowl.

Randy, now the senior minister at Oak Hills Church in San Antonio, recalled the story this way: He and his sister, Teresa, had been invited to Vacation Bible School at the Cleveland church when he was fourteen. Before the week was up, he'd become a Christian. The church was twenty minutes from his home, and it was up to Randy to find rides to and from church, for both morning and evening services. Rather than go home between services, it became easier to just hang out at the church or with friends who lived nearby. One of the teens he became friends with was Rozanne's brother. A friendship with Rozanne developed soon after that. "Rozanne had invited me over for an Italian dinner," Randy recalled. "I remember vividly the first time I was at a table when someone said grace, and it was with Rozanne's family. It was pretty profound . . . a defining moment for me."

Randy's family was unchurched, and there was nothing spiritual about mealtime at home. They didn't say grace, mostly, he says, because they all knew how hard his father worked at a blue-collar job to put food on the table. They thanked him—not God—for the food. "My dad got home at five o'clock and dinner was on the table at five thirty," Randy said. "We never had casseroles, and we never went out to eat. We always had dinner at the table, and we never had the TV on. Sunday would have been just one of the seven days a week we ate at home."

But when he went to the Bitonti home on Sundays, he knew immediately that something was very different. "I remember the four kids and her mom around the table, and her father said a prayer. He was a very gentle leader, and he said this prayer, and I remember looking up and thinking, 'Why is this grocer thanking God for the food?' I remember the faces of Rozanne's family; they were all smiling and there was something very different about that table experience versus what I had at home," Randy said. "I remember whispering a prayer: 'Dear God, I would like this for my family. One day I would like to get married and be that man and provide this for my children.' Then I ended up marrying his oldest daughter."

Soon Randy was spending more evenings at Rozanne's home, and he saw the difference her father made just by being home. He remembers Rozanne, her siblings, and her mother sitting down for an early meal. Her mother always saved a plate for her father, who came home later. When he sat at the table to eat his dinner, everyone returned to talk and listen. Randy knew instinctively that he wanted to become what he now believes every man should want to be: a leader at the family table, a presence who can speak volumes with only a few words. "It says a lot about a parent, particularly a father, who has the power to be a healing agent and bonding agent for his family," Randy said.

After high school, Rozanne and Randy went off to different colleges. They married during Randy's junior year and then Rozanne worked at a law firm to put him through Dallas Theological Seminary. Along the way, the couple had four children, Jennifer, David, Stephen, and Austin.

While Randy was in seminary, the family attended Pantego Bible Church in Fort Worth, where Randy volunteered as a Bible study leader. When Pantego's pastor left, attendance at Sunday services plummeted. But attendance at Randy's Bible study kept growing, so church elders asked him, at the age of twenty-eight, to become senior pastor. Over the next sixteen years, Randy Frazee grew that church by providing what he believed people craved: a sense of community.

It was his touch with small-group connections that caught the attention of the Willow Creek Community Church, a suburban Chicago megachurch. The Frazees headed to

Illinois, where they expected to stay for five to seven years, they said. But after just a couple of years, Max Lucado, the charismatic and very convincing pastor of Oak Hills, started calling. The Frazees' older kids had started college in Texas, so it wasn't hard to convince them to return south to pastor the San Antonio church.

The chronology of the Frazees' lives sounds simple enough—Ohio, Texas, Illinois, Texas. But along the way, the family made deep relationships with some amazing people and learned a lot about a universal longing for community. How the Frazees went from a family who made friends easily to a family whose very ministry revolved around building bonds in small groups hinged on a couple of outgoing neighbors and a bout with insomnia.

When the family still lived in the Dallas–Fort Worth area—in Arlington, actually— they became friends with Tom and Bonnie Erickson, a couple who knew everyone in their neighborhood. The Ericksons introduced them to people, showing the Frazees that they didn't just know names and faces, they knew people. They knew where they worked and where they were from. They knew what their hobbies were. They knew their kids' names and their pets' names. They knew what made their neighbors tick. "I'd say Tom had the gift of party, but I don't think he even drank," said Randy. "In Malcolm Gladwell's terms, Tom was a 'connector.' He pulled people in in a natural way."

Randy loves to tell a story about one Saturday morning, when he was mowing the lawn and went back indoors through the front door of his home to get a glass of water. He discovered Tom sitting in his living room, reading his paper. Stunned, he did the only thing he could think of: He offered to make a pot of coffee. "No, thanks," said Tom, holding up a mug of steaming coffee. "I already did."

Randy's initial reaction was that this neighbor might have a problem with boundaries— or that they might need to move. But through this interesting man, the Frazees began to understand what many others did not. Randy cites Will Miller's book *Refrigerator Rights: Creating Connections and Restoring Relationships*—a sociological study in the evolution of relationships— as he explains that most people don't want to be "hosted" when they're at the home of a friend, neighbor, or relative. If they're thirsty, they want to get a glass and help themselves. If they're hungry, they want to open the pantry and see what looks good. They may not want to make your mortgage payments, but they want to feel like your home is their home.

"Tom was the first person who taught me about refrigerator rights," said Randy. "In *Refrigerator Rights*, it says we don't need *more* relationships, but we need more relationships where people have been granted refrigerator rights."

It all intrigued Rozanne and Randy Frazee, who were working hard at Pantego Bible Church to build membership by creating a sense of community. When it came time for twice-monthly small-group gatherings at church, the Frazees would hire a sitter and drive for twenty minutes, passing by their neighbors who were walking, riding bikes, and talking in driveways. One day, they came to a startling conclusion: They wanted to stay home. "There we were waving good-bye to our neighbors, and one time I said, 'I don't want to go. I want to stay here," Rozanne said. "That night when we came home, we started talking about it and Randy said, 'I don't want to, either, but I'm the minister, and I *have* to go.'"

Randy Frazee remembered this busy time, too. He was working so hard to know church members better, but he saw them in this small-group setting just twice a month. The relationships weren't deep, and they didn't have anything close to the sense of community the Frazees had with their neighbors—people they saw sometimes organically and sometimes intentionally, from standing in their yards or at their mailboxes, to the neighborhood supermarket, or even at their children's schools. In the "aha moment" that followed, the Frazees realized it wouldn't be hard to juggle both. They'd drive to church for their small-group meetings that happened twice a month and still hold more frequent faith-based meetings in their Waggoner Street neighborhood. Rozanne would put on a pot of soup and invite in anyone and everyone. "We started a group with whoever wanted to be in it—you didn't have to go to our church—and we made some of the deepest relationships there. It was life-changing," Rozanne said. "We'd travel with neighbors, do mission trips with them—we just did life with them. It was so deep."

But somewhere along the way, Randy Frazee got lost. He'd been working all day, having dinner with his wife and children and then returning to meetings with church elders, long into the night. His family and neighborhood relationships lost some of their depth and Randy, who was about forty then, hit a wall. His life had become unbalanced: His family was still important to him, but it was not where he spent most of his time or energy. His church ministry was important, too, and it was sucking him dry emotionally and physically.

He couldn't sleep. Panic and fear set in. Finally, six weeks into significant sleep deprivation—not to mention anxiety and depression—he went to see a doctor. "This is a big story for me; it's my story of coming back to the table," Randy declared. "While I was really captured by the table experience with Rozanne's family when we were younger, I didn't value the experience when it was actually happening in our own family. I worked way too much, and I had moved away from my family."

"I went to a doctor who told me that if I wanted to stay off medication, I needed to find a rhythm to my life: Work during the day, relax at dusk, and sleep at night. It was a simple idea, but I still had to pay him for it," Randy said with a laugh.

The advice may have been common sense, but Randy Frazee took it seriously. He worked hard during the day, and at 6:00 p.m. he put his work down and didn't return to it until the next morning. He found himself with time on his hands and a wife eager to get reacquainted. "Now, all of a sudden, from six to ten p.m., I have four hours available every single night. That led us back to the dinner table. Essentially, the sequence had been Rozanne would cook for hours; we'd eat in twenty minutes and leave the table. The new equation became to linger, to 'recline at the table,' as it says in the Old Testament, and continue on with conversation."

During that lingering, the Frazee family built traditions—on weeknights and at Sunday dinners, Randy decided that the kids should share their day. They had to start with the basics, getting up in the morning and getting ready for school, and then eventually recount the more qualitative aspects of their lives. It might take the family forty-five minutes to get through the chronology, and if they had company, guests had to join in as well. At the end, each person rates the day, on a scale of one to ten. When the lingering is over, everyone helps clean up the kitchen, a task Randy and Rozanne have nicknamed the "Festival of the Cleanup."

Their Sunday dinners can run into the late afternoon hours and might end with everyone shifting to comfortable chairs in the backyard or smaller groups taking a walk and visiting with neighbors. They might rent a movie and gather around to watch. And as much as they occasionally enjoy eating outdoors in the backyard, sometimes Rozanne and Randy Frazee head elsewhere. Their front-yard adventures to get to know their neighbors began when Randy dug out a banjo his father had given him years ago. He grabbed a couple of chairs and started strumming in the front yard. Rozanne brought out a book and a chair and sat with him. Within a couple of weeks, curious neighbors started stopping by. The more chairs they added, the more people they met. Almost without realizing it, they had created something of a micropark in their own front yard. "I have a phrase," Randy said. "'I would like to waste the evening away with you.' Front-yard dwelling is our favorite thing to do, to see who God brings around."

The Frazees want to cure the nation—or at least the people they know in their neighborhood or reach through their church—of "crowded loneliness." They wrote *Real Simplicity* together as an ode to the dinner table, a place where fathers can be leaders, every person has a voice, and families who are believers can demonstrate their faith to those who are not. They host a monthly neighborhood potluck for believers from any church. Of the nearly 150 families in their neighborhood, thirty or more will take part in the gathering. "It's one of the things where you do an Evite and identify what needs to be brought. People respond, 'I'll bring the salad, or I'll bring the drinks,'" Randy said. "People are everywhere, and they absolutely love it."

If you are invited to dinner—on Sunday or any other day of the week—at the Frazees,' you will see how one family of Christians lives their faith. "Rozanne and I are neighborhood folk. We love the idea of applying the Biblical passage 'love your neighbor as yourself;' we take that literally," Randy said. "We want opportunities to encounter our neighbors on a regular basis," Randy said.

In their San Antonio neighborhood, it's a casual but intentional experience. When the family lived in the Chicago area, Frazee started the experience at Willow Creek Community Church, where he was a teaching pastor. They called it "the Table," and in homes all over that area, people came together at the dinner table. Buffet dinners weren't allowed; you had to have the experience of a family-style meal in which everyone worked to pass platters and bowls of food while sharing conversation.

"At some point in the dinner experience you share the highs and lows of your day," Randy said. "I remember in our home in our neighborhood, we had about forty in our little bungalow. We moved our furniture, and the most we could get around our table was twenty-seven, then we moved into the Boy Scout building."

When the *New York Times* got wind of it, a reporter was interested in attending one of the meals and writing about it. "She thought she was the first one there because there were no cars outside our house," Randy recalled. "I said, 'No, everyone walked. They all live here.' She was amazed."

For all of the effort that Randy Frazee has put into small-group ministry, what happens at the dinner table with the Frazees' children has set the pace for all else. Grace is the ritual that opens each meal and something Randy Frazee believes has affected his family tremendously, on a spiritual basis. "We've enjoyed a home filled with the presence of Christ. I've been in a lot of homes, and I can sense whether Christ is present. The thing we feel is transforming is that we have, day in and day out, invited Christ to be present in our home. We are ultimately not only thanking God for the food, but are also inviting Jesus to come to the table. It makes it a gathering in his name."

Like his father-in-law, Randy Frazee leads his family in prayer. "I always say the prayer because I read somewhere that it's more important for children to know who the head of the household is than the head of the country. I know that's old-fashioned," he said. Only on Randy's birthday does he hand that duty to someone else. "That's a really big deal. I almost always ask David, our oldest son. When I asked my son-in-law one time, I thought he was going to break down and cry."

Except when the meat is prepared on the grill outdoors, cooking is Rozanne's duty. While she's always looking for new recipes to try, the foundation of her culinary skills came from her mother.

It was the catalyst for me wanting to learn how to cook," Rozanne said. "I remember when my mom was pregnant with my youngest sister—I didn't know she was pregnant, I just knew she was sick—she was lying on the couch, really struggling.

"I went to her one night and said, 'Mom, I really want chicken cacciatore.' We had a little bungalow and the living room was small and the kitchen was small. I said, 'If you tell me how to make it, I think I can do it.' She gave me instructions from the couch, and I remember my dad taking his first bite and saying that it tasted just like Mom's." The delight she saw on her father's face that night and the warm feeling it gave her are what she tries to replicate in each meal she prepares.

The Frazees' children aren't really children anymore. Their daughter, Jennifer Lewis, is married and a mother, herself. Son David is in law school and is practically a newlywed. Stephen and Austin are both students at Baylor University in Waco, Texas. Their children are home together on most Sundays, and her daughter and son-in-law visit often. "We try to do five dinners a week together. I'll bet we get our daughter and her family at least three of those," said Rozanne.

Just as Rozanne's parents understood the need to know their children's friends, Rozanne and Randy do, too. When they went off to college, they made new friends and often brought them home to share their parents' dinner-table experience. And Jennifer noted that even after she and her brothers went off to college, their friends often stopped by to say hello to her parents and, if they just happened to stop in around dinnertime, they were more than happy to stay for a meal.

Their son David said that the first lesson it taught him was to understand the importance and value of being fully engaged in developing relationships with others—family or not. "Most kids come home and their parents are busy. They'll ask, 'How was your day?'

but they never stop multitasking," said David Frazee. "When we come in and they ask how our day was, we're sharing with someone who cares about us and loves us and we have their undivided attention."

Randy recalled Jennifer bringing home a friend who was profoundly affected by it. "Our daughter had grown up in a family that gathered around the table and always had neighbors over. She thought that was a common experience for everybody," he said. When she discovered it was not, she initially felt out of place.

Once she realized her new friends were curious, she took them home to meet her family. "There was one powerful experience when a girl came home with her. We're going around the table and sharing their day. All along the way Jennifer was talking to the girl, coaching her about how the conversation goes. When it came time for this girl to share her day, she got three to four sentences into it, and she started crying," Randy said. "When she finally regained her composure, she said, 'I've always wanted to be part of a family where I could share my day, I never knew how much I wanted it.' She was weeping because she wanted to be heard."

At that moment, Rozanne and Randy Frazee knew that their four children had witnessed the transformative powers that go with being part of something as strong and magical as a family. David assures them the lesson was not lost on him. "Sharing at the table was part of the experience in fostering an identity as a member of this family," he said. "It helped me shape into who I am in Christ. I'll always be a Frazee, and I'll always be a child of God."

David and his brothers all attended Baylor and headed off to college already knowing how to make the Bitonti family pasta. They still practiced discussing the elements of their day, just like they did in San Antonio.

"When they went away to college, they started to miss that," Randy said. "Eating is not only for refueling—that would be barbaric. It's the coming around the table in conversation. That is one of the things families are really missing—they don't have conversation. We have raised a family, and I'm not bragging, because those first years I was absolutely absent from my family. We have been characters in one another's story, and every night we read a new page and every day a page turns."

Frazee may have been absent for a while, but his kids will be the first to tell you that he's made up for it since. They are acutely aware of the home life their parents created for them and the love they shared with neighbors and others. "My parents have never met a stranger.

They are there for everyone around them," Jennifer said. "I know that the love we had in our family can extend to the people next door and it can have a big impact on them."

For families who recognize what's missing but don't know how or where to start, Rozanne and Randy have simple advice: Ask them how their day was. "We talk to people who say, 'My kids aren't interested in that.' I tell them, 'You're mistaken,'" Randy said.

Randy Frazee has been a minister to congregations of thousands for three decades. He's written books and is known for navigating groups large and small. But he knows where his real strength lies. "If you were to talk to people who have known us in the Dallas–Fort Worth area, Chicago, or San Antonio, I think people would say, 'They have brought us back to the table.' I think that would be strong enough to be etched in our epitaph," Randy said with a laugh. "Other people say their pastor brought them to Jesus, I brought them back to the table."

ABOUT THE FRAZEE FAMILY

THEIR CHURCH: Oak Hills Church, San Antonio, Texas

DENOMINATION: Nondenominational

ATTENDANCE: More than 8,000 attend weekly services.

THEIR ROLES: Randy Frazee is senior minister, partnering at Oak Hills with pastor and author Max Lucado

THEIR FAMILY: The Frazees have four children: daughter Jennifer Lewis (husband Desmond), and sons David (wife Gretchen), Stephen, and Austin. They have one granddaughter, Ava.

COMMUNITY OUTREACH: On the national stage: Randy Frazee is a frequent speaker on community ministry. His latest project is "The Story," done with his co-pastor Rev. Max Lucado and several Christian contemporary singers.

READ MORE: Rozanne and Randy Frazee are the authors of *Real Simplicity*. Randy is the author of *The Christian Life Profile Assessment*, *Making Room for Life: Trading Chaotic Lifestyles for Connected Relationships*, and *The Connecting Church* (with Larry Crabb, George Gallup, and Dallas Willard). To learn more about the Frazees and Oak Hills Church, go to oakhillschurch.com or randyfrazee.com.

Pulled Pork Sandwiches

{ Serves 10 }

This easy-to-make entrée is a no-brainer for any family. You can assemble the dish in minutes, and eight hours later you've got tender sandwich meat in a rich, barbecue-y sauce.

3 pounds pork loin

1 (12- to 16-ounce) bottle Italian salad dressing

1 (12- to 16-ounce) bottle barbecue sauce

8 to 10 buns

1 medium-size yellow onion, sliced, for serving

Place the pork loin in a shallow dish or resealable plastic bag and cover with the salad dressing. Cover and marinate overnight in the refrigerator.

Place the pork loin and the dressing in a slow cooker and cook on the LOW setting for 8 hours or on HIGH for 4 hours.

For the last 30 minutes of cooking, add the barbecue sauce. (If there is a lot of juice after cooking, drain some of it off before covering with the barbecue sauce.)

Remove the pork loin from the slow cooker and place it in a shallow baking dish or on a cutting board. Remove any excess fat, then pull apart the meat using two forks. Spoon the barbecue sauce over the pork and stir well.

Serve the pulled pork on buns with onions and extra barbecue sauce from the slow cooker.

Pulled Pork Tacos

{ Serves 10 }

Fire-roasted tomatoes and savory seasonings combine to make a meaty filling that's so flavorful you may not want to use toppings on your taco. And this recipe works just as well with chicken or beef.

3 pounds boneless Boston pork butt roast

1 (28-ounce) can whole fire-roasted tomatoes

1 (14-ounce) can crushed fire-roasted tomatoes

1 chipotle pepper

1 tablespoon adobo sauce

1 medium-size yellow onion, minced

2 teaspoons salt

½ teaspoon freshly ground black pepper

1 teaspoon dried oregano

2 bay leaves

Corn or flour tortillas, for serving

Sour cream, for serving

1 bunch fresh cilantro, for serving

Shredded Cheddar or Monterey Jack cheese, for serving

Lime slices, for serving

Put the pork roast in a slow cooker, then add both cans of tomatoes.

Mince the chipotle pepper and add it and the adobo sauce to the slow cooker. Add the onion, salt, pepper, oregano, and bay leaves. Cover the slow cooker and cook on HIGH for 4 hours or on LOW for 8 hours.

Remove the roast from the slow cooker and place it in a shallow baking dish or on a cutting board. Remove any excess fat, then pull apart the meat using two forks.

Serve the pulled pork on tortillas with sour cream, cilantro, cheese, and the juice from the lime slices.

Asparagus with Balsamic Tomatoes

··{ Serves 6 }··

The aromatic tomato-based topping for this asparagus side dish is so good you'll want to serve it over all kinds of vegetables. Rozanne Frazee found this healthy recipe in *Cooking Light* magazine.

1 pound asparagus, trimmed

2 teaspoons extra-virgin olive oil

1⅓ cups halved grape tomatoes

1 teaspoon minced fresh garlic

2 tablespoons balsamic vinegar

¼ teaspoon salt

½ teaspoon freshly ground black pepper

4 tablespoons crumbled goat cheese

Steam the asparagus, or cook it in boiling water for 2 minutes or until crisp-tender. Drain and set aside.

In a large skillet, heat the olive oil over medium-high heat. Add the tomatoes and garlic to the skillet; cook about 5 minutes. Stir in the vinegar; cook 3 minutes. Stir in the salt and pepper.

Arrange the asparagus on a platter and top it with the tomato mixture. Sprinkle with the goat cheese and serve.

Amaretto Flan with Summer Fruit

{ Serves 6 to 8 }

Fresh fruit is the perfect accompaniment for this light, almond-flavored dessert.

½ cup sugar

1 (14-ounce) can sweetened condensed milk

3 large eggs

3 large egg yolks

1 cup half-and-half

½ cup amaretto

Sliced peaches, apricots, strawberries, kiwis, or berries, for serving

Preheat the oven to 350°F.

Sprinkle the sugar in a 9-inch round cake pan and place it on the stovetop over medium heat. Using oven mitts, caramelize the sugar by shaking the pan occasionally until the sugar melts and turns a light golden brown; set aside to cool. (The mixture may crack slightly as it cools.)

In a large bowl, combine the sweetened condensed milk, eggs, egg yolks, half-and-half, and amaretto and beat at high speed with an electric mixer for 15 seconds.

Pour the egg mixture over the caramelized sugar. Cover the pan tightly with foil and place it in a larger shallow pan. Pour hot water to a depth of 1 inch in the larger pan so that it surrounds the flan pan.

Bake for 55 minutes. Carefully remove the flan cake pan from the water and uncover it immediately.

Allow the flan to cool for at least 30 minutes, then remove it from the pan by loosening the edges of the flan with a spatula. Invert the pan onto a larger serving plate and allow the caramel sauce to drip down the sides of the flan.

Serve with fresh fruit.

Strawberry Salad with Vinaigrette

{ Serves 8 to 10 }

Monterey Jack cheese, berries, and pecans stir the senses in this terrific salad. The garlic and paprika in the dressing make it a standout you'll want to have in your pantry all the time.

SALAD

1 head romaine lettuce

1 head Bibb lettuce

½ cup shredded Monterey Jack cheese

2 cups strawberries, hulled and halved

½ cup pecans or walnuts

VINAIGRETTE

1 cup vegetable oil

¾ cup superfine sugar

¾ cup red wine vinegar

2 cloves garlic, minced

½ teaspoon salt

½ teaspoon paprika

¼ teaspoon ground white pepper

MAKE THE SALAD: Tear the lettuce into pieces and place it in a large bowl.

Sprinkle the top of the salad with the cheese. Arrange the strawberry halves on top of the salad and then sprinkle with nuts.

MAKE THE VINAIGRETTE: Whisk the oil, sugar, vinegar, garlic, salt, paprika, and pepper until the sugar is dissolved. (You can also place all the ingredients in a jar or container with a lid and shake until it's combined.)

Drizzle the dressing over the salad and toss well.

CHAPTER NINE

Rev. Kirbyjon and Pastor Suzette

Caldwell

{ Windsor Village United Methodist Church ∞ Houston, Texas }

God is great; God is good.

Let us thank Him for our food.

By His hand, we are fed.

Thank You for our daily bread.

In Jesus' name, amen.

(And bless the cook!)

FAMILY BRINGS SENSE OF COMMUNITY

When Kirbyjon Caldwell was just a little boy, his father brought Tina Turner home for dinner one evening. When Kirbyjon's bedtime rolled around, the famous singer tucked him in and kissed him goodnight before turning out his bedroom light and returning to his parents' living room.

The entertainer was a hot nightclub act and was in Houston to perform at the Crystal White Hotel. Much of America was still segregated then, and the hotel was the nicest place in the city for African Americans to stay. Its nightclub was open until the wee hours and drew big-name acts such as Ike and Tina Turner, Ray Charles, B. B. King, James Brown, and Patti LaBelle. Kirbyjon's father, Booker T. Caldwell, owned a tailor shop next door to the hotel, so visiting nightclub acts and other black VIPs who came through town often stopped in for his ready-to-wear and custom-made suits.

Over the years they all became friends with the elder Caldwell, who could spot a visitor in need of a home-cooked meal. He knew his heart was open and that, with a little notice, his wife's kitchen would be as well.

The Reverend Kirbyjon Caldwell, now senior pastor at Windsor Village United Methodist Church, the largest United Methodist church in the country, with sixteen thousand members, was raised by parents with very different family dynamics. His mother, Jean, an only child, grew up a city girl. His father, Booker T., was one of thirteen children and was raised on a farm in the country. But their values were the same: Education, hard work, good manners and respect for others were all important. They were both raised to be responsible to their families and understood that each generation should do better than the last. All of this was passed on to their son as well as their daughter, Dorothea Pickens, who also lives in the Houston area.

And when family and friends came together, good food and conversation flowed. "I was brought up in a Christian family who believed in *family*," recalled Jean Caldwell. Her father worked as a butler and worked most Sundays. So when he got a Sunday off, that made for a very special day. A big meal with aunts, uncles, cousins, and grandparents was a sure thing. "We loved to eat, but we ate healthy, nutritious food. My dad had hypertension as a young man, and if a doctor had told him to eat nails to get better, he would have tried it," she said. "Pork was a no-no. Anything fried was a no-no."

Jean and Booker T. met as students at Prairie View University; she was an education major and he was an agriculture major. They landed in Houston partly because Jean's parents and extended family were there and partly because a big city simply held more promise for a young couple just getting started in life together.

When Kirbyjon was born in 1953, Booker T. was busy establishing his business and Jean was busy teaching, going to school, and participating in church activities. Her parents lived just down the street from them and were a constant presence in their lives, particularly when it came to being together for dinner—Sundays and on other days—and connecting as a family.

The children grew up in a neighborhood that lived the philosophy that it takes a village to raise a child. If any child misbehaved while out playing, his parents knew about it before he ever got home.

Boys in the neighborhood often played ball in the street and, said Jean Caldwell, Kirbyjon often had to leave games before they were over. When dinner was ready, it was time to come home. "I would be outside playing, and my grandmother would call me in. I can still hear her: 'Kir-r-r-by'—that's what they called me then—'it's time to eat,'" he mimicked in a sing-song voice. "When a cold front comes in, it makes me think of her soups—her gumbo and chili," he said one cool fall morning. Then he drifted into childhood memories of his grandmother, rattling off her comfort-food meals—fried chicken, macaroni and cheese, homemade rolls, hearty soups, and cobblers—with a smile on his face. "I grew up in a nurturing, loving family, and my extended family encouraged me, corrected me, and disciplined me," said Kirbyjon. "There was hardly a day that I felt unloved, and that means a lot. But I didn't know what that meant until I got older."

Along the way, Kirbyjon gathered business and social skills that would later serve him well. He had a paper route and learned to approach people, collect money, and follow through on his responsibility to deliver the news. Helping out in his father's retail business, he learned about salesmanship and life in general, his father said. "He was a better salesman than I was," the elder Caldwell observed in an interview before his death in 2011. "We had everyone—from bankers to con men and pimps—coming in. Kirbyjon was equally polite to all. They all loved him."

When Kirbyjon went off to college it was not to become a man of the cloth, but to be a businessman. He eventually earned an MBA from the University of Pennsylvania's Wharton School of Business, but after a few years of work on Wall Street and as a bond broker, he was restless. When he approached his parents about returning to school—Southern Methodist University's Perkins School of Theology seminary would be his next destination—they knew he could do it, they just weren't sure how he'd earn a living at it. "I was concerned because preachers traded with me, but they didn't buy many clothes, and they often bought them on credit," said Booker T. with a laugh, still weighing the practicalities of life choices well into his eighties.

Kirbyjon Caldwell served as an associate pastor at Methodist churches in Dallas and then Houston until 1982, when he was made senior pastor of Windsor Village United Methodist Church. It had just twenty-five members and a fair amount of debt—by all accounts, this church was on its last leg. But Kirbyjon was determined to succeed, and over the next three decades, he and his wife, Suzette, grew it into the largest United Methodist congregation in the United States. Their ministry approach is holistic, his business background influencing everything from church administration to the community around him. Workshops at the church can range from teaching financial responsibility to helping families with special-needs children. Their church obligations run far beyond regularly scheduled services. Windsor Village's strongest mission work serves its own neighborhood. It has developed a 234-acre subdivision for mostly first-time homebuyers just across the street from the church. They've also worked at developing businesses—including franchise restaurants and other retail establishments. They were instrumental in getting a public library built in the neighborhood and even opened charter schools, one of them named after Kirbyjon's mother, Jean Hines-Caldwell, a longtime teacher and counselor at Phillis Wheatley High School in Houston. "I'm amazed at what God has built through him," Jean Caldwell said of her son. "It's only through God that that would have been done. It's amazing. If you listen to His word, anyone can do the same thing."

Kirbyjon is a dynamic preacher in the pulpit and a leader on the Houston civic scene as well. On the national stage, he gave the benediction at both inaugurations for President George W. Bush and quietly served as a spiritual counselor during the president's eight years in office. When Bush's daughter Jenna married in 2008, Caldwell was called on to officiate.

But back in Houston, Kirbyjon and Suzette Caldwell take their church duties seriously, their personalities and strengths complementing one another. Whereas Kirbyjon is outgoing and charismatic, Suzette is more quiet and thoughtful. Her specialty is prayer, and she is board chair and president of the Prayer Institute, a nonprofit created by Windsor Village and committed to praying for people and teaching people about the power of prayer. In the Bible study they teach together, the Caldwells' down-to-earth demeanors create an environment in which group members can be open, even vulnerable. But when Suzette takes the podium, this soft-spoken former engineer ignites.

On Sundays, the Caldwell family is at the sprawling church complex until well past a traditional lunchtime, so family dinner time is an evening meal. After all the "amens" and handshakes are over, Suzette heads home with their three children—Turner, Nia, and Alex—while Kirbyjon ties up loose ends. Her first stop is the supermarket for fresh meat and produce. Then she heads home for family time. This tight-knit and lively family makes it a priority that Sunday afternoons and evenings are spent together. Even if one of the children has a sports practice or game, whatever happens, happens as a family.

If they're free of soccer or baseball games, the Caldwells ride bikes, play Ping-Pong, or jump on the trampoline in their backyard. A favorite—and healthy—meal comes from marinating chicken in a "concoction" Suzette throws together—olive oil, lemon juice, and loads of fragrant herbs and spices—and then the rest of the family pitches in to produce the rest of their Sunday dinner. Corn on the cob or baked sweet potatoes are often easy side dishes.

Kitchen duty is shared by all. While Suzette does most of the cooking, Kirbyjon, who is known to make a mean mac 'n' cheese, pitches in, too. The children help set the table and always make their own salads so they're prepared exactly as they like them. Eldest son Turner is a budding cook. His cousin Sheldon, who's in his twenties and is a chef, has had an impact on the young man, who wants to learn how to prepare the foods he likes to eat. That means he's gotten handy at making omelets and all kinds of shrimp dishes.

When the food is prepared and the table set, the Caldwells sit down to pray, eat, and connect. "As a relatively older dad, I am particularly aware of being involved in their lives. I want to keep the door of communication open through their teen years and the rest of their lives," said Kirbyjon. "When life is testy to them, later and always, I want them to know they can come to Mom and Dad."

Granted, their children are young and still centered on home life, but Kirbyjon and Suzette hope that the close bonds they've built will remain with their children forever.

One thing they agree on now is that birthdays are special. They—and the treats that go with them—have evolved into the "it" family celebration here. Perhaps it's also a function of the children's ages that birthdays are so important. The childlike wonder of having a special day filled with all their favorite things is hard for adults to resist as well.

When one of the children is approaching his or her big day, they go into full birthday mode. Weeks of thought go into preparation: What kind of cake will they have? Will they have a special meal at home or dine out? Which celebrations will happen on the actual birthday and which are more likely to get extended-family Sunday dinner treatment? What will they take to share with classmates at school? And who will be invited to the "friends" birthday party?

Birthday boys or girls—whether parent or child—wake up to a big "Happy Birthday" sign and balloons tied to their chair at the dining room table. That evening, they'll have a small family celebration. Then comes the extended family celebration with grandparents, aunts, uncles, and cousins—sometimes at home, other times in a restaurant. There's a birthday celebration at school, and a party at home with friends. All, of course, showcase the favorite meals and treats of each birthday boy or girl.

As Kirbyjon and Suzette laugh about the many ways their children can extend the special treatment that comes with a birthday, Kirbyjon pauses to talk about another reason birthdays are so important: There was a time Suzette wondered whether there would be many more for her. In 2003, she found a lump in a monthly breast self-exam. A few medical tests later, and she was bound for surgery to address the cancer that was discovered early but nevertheless was an aggressive form of the disease. Since then, she's dedicated herself to a healthy lifestyle of wholesome foods and exercise—she works out with a trainer and hits the pool in a master swim program—and it's impossible for Kirbyjon and the kids not to follow. More than five years post diagnosis and treatment, Suzette is considered cancer free. But the scare of an uncertain future brought clarity and resolve to this couple whose faith was already unwavering.

Whether it's a weeknight meal or a special occasion, no meal is eaten—at home or in a restaurant—without first saying grace. Both Kirbyjon and Suzette pray frequently—asking for strength, expressing thanks for each and every day. But each meal begins with the same words: the "God is great, God is good . . ." prayer, spoken in unison. It's a simple prayer children can learn when they're young, with a little kick at the end—"And bless the cook!"

When the prayer is said and plates are full, the family connects. They talk about events of the day, what happened at work and at school. Sure, conversations happen all day long, in person and over the phone, in the car or at home. But dinnertime is when the three Caldwell children know they have their parents' undivided attention. "There are a lot of single parents out there and parents working very long hours," Kirbyjon said with broad gestures. "You have to ask yourselves what's most important. It's your choice."

Suzette believes good parenting is about establishing both respect and boundaries: "We want to give our children the space to express themselves, but there must be a boundary because they must respect us. We work at parenting our children; we are not trying to be their friends. We are not concerned about whether they *like* us, but we do want them to *love* us."

That caring nature not only gave Kirbyjon and Suzette a sense of security, it also gave them a sense of history. Suzette grew up in Arkansas amid lots of relatives. Her parents, Gussie Turner and Fred Turner Jr., divorced when she was twelve, so "home" was her grandmother, mother, and sister, Debbye Turner Bell, who was Miss America 1990. Regular family dinners involved just the four women, but when they visited her father's side of the family, things were different. "On my dad's side, there were lots of people. We'd all get together for a big family event, and after we ate, the adults would be in the living room talking and laughing. People would play games, dominoes, Scrabble, and cards," she said of the four-generation gatherings.

For all the eating and talking and laughing, the gatherings frequently culminated in the adults rehashing old times. They'd reminisce about their childhood and escapades of relatives long gone. Aunts and uncles talked about relatives who'd passed, and they always mentioned Suzette's great-grandmother Lila Turner, the daughter of slaves freed in the Emancipation. Suzette remembers Lila Turner as a formidable woman who had seventeen children and even after she'd gone blind still did all of the cooking and cleaning and walked to church by herself. She'd sit on her front porch and greet neighbors, recognizing them by the sound of their footsteps.

Suzette's ancestors were slaves in Burleson County, Texas, and continued to work the fields there after they were freed. "We are very proud of our heritage," she said. "We come from people who worked hard and were strong and loyal and worked for nothing when they were slaves."

ABOUT THE CALDWELL FAMILY

THEIR CHURCH: Windsor Village United Methodist Church, Houston, Texas

DENOMINATION: United Methodist Church

ATTENDANCE: 16,000 members

THEIR ROLES: Kirbyjon Caldwell is senior pastor; Suzette Caldwell is associate pastor and CEO of its Kingdom Builders Prayer Institute.

THEIR FAMILY: The Caldwells have three children: sons Turner and Alex, and daughter Nia.

COMMUNITY OUTREACH: Through Windsor Village, the Caldwells encourage economic empowerment to church members and the nearby community. In addition to Patrice House, a shelter for abused children, a nonprofit established by WVUMC created Corinthian Pointe, a subdivision of more than 200 acres. At the height of the current economic depression, not one homeowner defaulted on a mortgage. They have established two charter schools and recruited many businesses to open in the area.

ON THE NATIONAL STAGE: Kirbyjon Caldwell, a spiritual adviser to President George W. Bush, gave the benediction at Bush's 2001 and 2005 inaugurations. He also officiated at the 2008 wedding of Bush's daughter Jenna.

READ MORE: Kirbyjon Caldwell is the author of *Be in It to Win It*, *Entrepreneurial Faith*, and *The Gospel of Good Success*. Suzette Caldwell is the author of *Praying to Change Your Life*. To learn more about the Caldwells and Windsor Village United Methodist Church, go to kingdombuilders.com.

Marinated Grilled Chicken

{ Serves 4 }

The marinade for this recipe—which Suzette Caldwell calls her "concoction"—can be altered to suit any family's tastes. If your herb garden is overflowing with basil or oregano, chop it up and add to taste. Prefer the flavor of rosemary? That works just fine. As a marinade, this recipe is very forgiving—you simply cannot mess it up. In fact, you may want to keep a bottle of it in your pantry because it tastes great on salad, too.

½ cup olive oil

½ cup freshly squeezed lemon juice

¼ cup chopped fresh parsley

2 cloves garlic, pressed

1 teaspoon sea salt

1 teaspoon freshly ground black pepper

4 boneless, skinless chicken breast halves

Mix the oil, lemon juice, parsley, garlic, salt, and pepper in a small bowl. Transfer the marinade to a resealable plastic bag and add the chicken. Seal tightly and refrigerate for at least 2 hours.

Preheat an outdoor grill to medium. Place the chicken breasts on the grill and cook for 10 to 12 minutes on each side. When the chicken is done, transfer to a platter and serve immediately.

{ NOTE }

If you don't like grilled meat, follow the above recipe but bake it in your oven at 350°F for 45 minutes, or until done.

Old-Fashioned Macaroni and Cheese
························{ Serves 12 }························

This luscious dish isn't necessarily a regular menu item for this health-conscious family, but when they've just got to have some old-fashioned comfort food, Kirbyjon Caldwell hits the kitchen to make this special recipe the way his mother made it.

8 ounces large elbow macaroni

Olive oil

½ cup (1 stick) butter

¼ cup chopped fresh chives

1 (12-ounce) can evaporated milk

1 teaspoon salt

16 ounces shredded mild Cheddar cheese

Preheat the oven to 350°F. Grease a 3-quart baking dish.

Bring a large pot of water to a boil. Add the macaroni and a sprinkle of olive oil. Cook until al dente. Drain and set aside.

Melt the butter in a medium-size saucepan. Add the chives, evaporated milk, and salt and stir well.

Place half of the macaroni in the prepared baking dish. Cover with half of the cheese. Layer with the remaining macaroni and top with the remaining cheese. Pour the milk mixture over the top.

Bake for 20 minutes, or until the milk mixture is absorbed. Turn on the broiler for 1 to 2 minutes to brown the top of the cheese.

Green Apple Walnut Salad

{ Serves 4 to 6 }

Although their children are fussier about their salads, this is the side dish Suzette and Kirbyjon Caldwell like to eat.

1 head romaine lettuce

1 cup diced Granny Smith apple

½ cup walnut pieces

½ cup dried cranberries (set a little aside for topping)

5 ounces crumbled Gorgonzola cheese (set a little aside for topping)

½ cup Girard's Champagne Dressing

Chop the end off the head of lettuce, then rinse the leaves in cold water. Tear the lettuce into small pieces and place half of it into a large salad bowl. Set the remainder of the lettuce pieces aside.

Sprinkle half of the diced apples, walnut pieces, dried cranberries, and crumbled Gorgonzola cheese over the lettuce in the salad bowl. Toss to mix. After mixing well, add the remaining lettuce and the other half of the fruit, nuts, and cheese. Mix the entire bowl of salad until the ingredients are thoroughly blended. Sprinkle a few dried cranberries and extra Gorgonzola cheese on top of the salad for color.

Pour the dressing on the salad mixture and toss. Serve immediately.

Cinnamon-Raisin Biscuits

{ Serves 12 }

The key to these flaky biscuits is using very cold butter and cream and working the dough as little as possible. Suzette Caldwell started with a basic biscuit recipe, then added sugar, cinnamon, and raisins to take these from savory to sweet.

4 cups all-purpose flour, plus more for dusting

2 tablespoons baking powder

1 teaspoon coarse salt

5 tablespoons sugar

1 teaspoon ground cinnamon

1 cup (2 sticks) unsalted butter, cut into pieces

2 cups heavy cream

1 cup raisins

1 cup confectioners' sugar

3 tablespoons whole milk

Preheat the oven to 400°F. Line a baking sheet with parchment paper.

In a large bowl, whisk together the flour, baking powder, salt, sugar, and cinnamon. Using a pastry blender or fork, cut in the butter until the mixture resembles coarse crumbs. Add the cream and stir just until the dough comes together. (The mixture will be sticky.) Add the raisins and incorporate into the dough gently and quickly.

Transfer the dough to a lightly floured work surface and, with floured fingers, knead the dough until it forms a ball. Sprinkle flour on the work surface and lightly dust the dough to keep it from sticking.

Using a rolling pin, roll out the dough to a 1-inch thickness. Use a biscuit or cookie cutter to cut out biscuits. Place the biscuits on the prepared baking sheet and bake for 18 to 20 minutes, or until lightly browned.

To make a glaze, sift the confectioners' sugar into a small mixing bowl, then add the milk 1 tablespoon at a time until you reach a thin, but not runny, consistency.

Allow the biscuits to cool for a few minutes, then top with the glaze and serve while they're still warm.

Spritz Cookies

{ Makes 4 dozen cookies }

Suzette Caldwell says this pressed-cookie recipe is a favorite of hers. With a buttery, melt-in-your-mouth texture, just one can cure her craving for something sweet. Her children enjoy lending a hand, adding food coloring and topping with candies such as sprinkles, Red Hots, or even chocolate chips.

1 cup (2 sticks) butter, softened

½ cup sugar

Food coloring (optional)

1 large egg

1 teaspoon almond extract

2¼ cups all-purpose flour

½ teaspoon salt

Candies, for decorating (optional)

Preheat the oven to 400°F.

In a large bowl, mix the butter and sugar until smooth. Add food coloring one drop at a time as desired, then blend until the butter mixture reaches a uniform color. Add the egg and almond extract and blend.

Sift together the flour and salt, then gradually add the dry ingredients to the butter mixture. Cover the bowl with plastic wrap and refrigerate for at least 1 hour, until firm.

Place the dough in a cookie press; form the desired shapes on an ungreased baking sheet.

Place the candies or other decoration on the top of the pressed cookies. Bake the cookies until they are set but not browned, 6 to 9 minutes. Remove immediately from the baking sheet and let cool on a wire rack.

CHAPTER TEN

Pastors Matthew and Caroline
Barnett

·······{ Angelus Temple and the Dream Center ❧ Los Angeles, California }·······

Dear Heavenly Father,
we thank You for this meal that You have given us, and we praise
Your name for all of the blessings in our lives. I pray that You would
keep Your hand on this family and this household. May we live
our lives as an example of Your love. May every person we meet
and every opportunity that presents itself open a door to show
the world Your love. I pray for all of the hurting people of our city.
Help us find a way to uplift them and alleviate their pain as we go
about our lives this week. We thank You for this time we can spend
together, and may we grow ever closer as a family, always showing gratitude
for what You have given us. Let us live our lives in constant celebration
of Your goodness. Give us the strength to build Your kingdom,
and a peace of mind knowing that we can trust in You in all things. Let us
not give in to discouragement or fatigue, and let us always be striving
to honor You even more.
Your grace and Your love are always with us.
In Your precious name we pray, amen.

DINNER IS A TIME TO HIT THE RESET BUTTON

When Matthew Barnett transports himself back to his childhood in Phoenix, it's filled with memories of a busy Christ-centered home that revolved around the work of his famous father, Rev. Tommy Barnett, who has created two megachurches, cofounded the Dream Center outreach ministry, and helped countless other pastors to be leaders in their faith and civic communities.

Weekdays were noisy and interesting, he said, but Sundays were special. His mother, Marja, would get up early to get her family ready for services at Phoenix First Assembly of God, which today is one of the top ten largest churches in the country and draws more than sixteen thousand to services each week, according to Lifeway's annual church report. She'd also get dinner started, so it would be piping hot and super spicy by the time they got home. "Every Sunday we ate the same thing: steaming hot curry made with curry powder sent by my aunt, who was a missionary in India, so it was authentic," Matthew said. "I was a little kid so I had no choice. I'd go home and have to force fire—red hot, super fire—down my throat. My dad loved the heat; he'd almost put Tabasco on it. I remember Dad's getting excited on Saturday nights that he was going to have curry on Sunday. He'd talk about it on the way home from church. Being the youngest, I enjoyed the food the least, but I enjoyed the fact that we were there together."

That was back in the late 1970s, and his mom thought that they could be more relaxed and have more fun if they ate in the living room rather than around the kitchen or dining room table. So they'd sit cross-legged on the living room floor, say a quick prayer, and then eat their curry and rice and talk. "Those were great times," Matthew reminisced. "There was never a distinction that church was one thing and home another. Church was our life, and we all loved it. We'd talk about the day and encourage Dad about how the sermon went. He'd wonder if he'd hit this too hard or missed that and we made a point to build him up."

At some point in the afternoon, Matthew's friends—either from church or the high school basketball team on which he played—would stop by. It wasn't uncommon for them to walk in the back door as if they lived there, check out what was in the fridge, or just grab a box of Lucky Charms and eat the cereal straight out of the box. "My mom wanted our home to be a welcoming place rather than a place to avoid," Matthew said. "She realized that boys are so different growing up and the camaraderie is so different. Mom rolled with it; she was cool that way."

Extended family members were in Kansas City, and every visit meant a stop at Arthur Bryant's Barbecue for a heart-stopping stack of sliced beef with tangy sauce on top of sliced white bread. Matthew grew up eating many of the same foods his father did, because even though Marja Barnett's Swedish heritage influenced what came out of her kitchen, her mother-in-law taught her to make Tommy's favorites. To this day, Matthew thinks of his grandmother and mother when he eats pecan pie or biscuits and gravy, not to mention Swedish meatballs. Tacos and tostadas were added to the repertoire after Tommy and Marja Barnett moved their family to Arizona.

Tommy Barnett talked to his three children—Matthew as well as his older siblings, Luke and Kristie—about concepts such as what faith, dedication, and serving God meant and then let them make their own choices. "Dad gave me a compelling vision of God," Matthew said.

In September 1994, Tommy Barnett drove his youngest son—then just twenty—to Los Angeles and dropped him off in the city's impoverished Echo Park district. The streets were populated by pimps and prostitutes, drug addicts and dealers, and people with a host of problems and nowhere to go. Those were exactly the people the Barnetts were after. "They say if you can reach the people no one wants, you'll get the people everyone wants," Matthew said.

A few years later, Matthew found his calling in Los Angeles, taking over as the preacher at the aging Angelus Temple, the birthplace of the International Church of the Foursquare Gospel. The once-dying Angelus Temple now draws five thousand people to its services each week.

With his father as his mentor, he also founded the Dream Center in a former hospital. It has grown into a massive outreach that touches forty-five thousand people a month. It helps addicts through recovery; gives a home to runaways; and provides food, clothing, and a safe haven for the needy and the homeless.

In the center's early days, Matthew was a young, single guy who had no staff, no friends, and an enormous task in front of him. He took it one day at a time, and reached the people of the street on their level. "I found my joy eating at the taco trucks. I'd get one taco for fifty cents, then maybe two. I'd hang out and talk to the local guys on Sunset Boulevard—those were the people who originally came to my church," he said.

As the Dream Center and church found success, they drew more people to religious services, and volunteers—regular folks and Hollywood celebrities alike—showed up in droves.

They brought energy, ideas, and a passion for helping others. One of those volunteers was Caroline Olsson, who understood what it was like to go through hard times and wanted to help deliver food to the needy. Caroline was just two when her parents, Anja and Clarence Olsson, packed up their four young daughters and left Sweden for the United States. They didn't speak English, but Clarence wanted to sell beautiful Swedish crystal chandeliers in America, a country of wealth and opportunity. A recession hit the U.S. economy in the early 1980s, and the family's hopes for success were dashed. Her father took whatever work he could find. At night, they all ate dinner together and the four Olsson daughters talked about everything under the sun. "My fondest memories growing up were around the dinner table. I ate at home all the time, and we used that time to connect," Caroline said.

When Matthew and Caroline met, he knew right away that Caroline was special, and by 1999 the couple married. They now have two children, daughter Mia and son Caden. When they married, Caroline figured she'd be cooking every night, but Matthew's just not cut that way. "Matthew loves to be out and about, around people and their energy. He's never met a stranger; he has that gift. He can be anywhere and talk to anyone," she said.

Caroline's mother has always been fascinated by food and loves to watch cooking shows on TV. Even when there wasn't much money, Anja managed to prepare delicious meals on a small budget. Caroline remembers her mother's pot roast, potatoes, and cucumber salad, as well as a cake with strawberries and whipped cream. That was their "Sunday cake." Everything, of course, was made from scratch.

A few years ago the Olssons moved in with Caroline and Matthew, and Anja does most of the cooking. Matthew raved about his mother-in-law's cooking—many of her Swedish dishes reminded him of his mother's cooking. "My mother-in-law is the biggest gourmet chef of all time. She lives with us and makes unbelievable meals. We have rack of lamb once a week—oh, my goodness, it's so good. We might have Korean barbecue another night; she's a very international cook."

On Sundays after church, they go home for dinner. "It's usually a five-course meal," said Matthew. "It's like she's trying to win an award every single Sunday."

Caroline said dinner was a special time when she was growing up, and she wanted to re-create that for her children, too. "There's just something about sitting around the table and talking about your day. It puts a reset button on your life."

Dinner starts with a prayer, composed to "remember who's in control of our lives," Matthew said. He believes time spent around the table can be filled with life-changing moments. He asks the diners what they learned in church, and the kids get to ask questions, too. Most of their questions are experience based, such as asking about why people are homeless or why the church helps certain people. If the Dream Center's outreach teams have brought in a new family to the shelter, they may talk about that. "They get a big perspective of life," Matthew said. "We encourage them to join in with us."

Often it's just family, but it's not uncommon for the kids to bring friends home from church. Then they just hang out together the rest of the day. On Sunday nights, the kids go to bed around eight thirty and Caroline and Matthew get a date night. "I love what we created on Sunday afternoons, a time to be together," Matthew said.

One night a week, Matthew lets his children pick their dinner destination. It might be Chuck E. Cheese or Dave & Busters, where they can hang out, play video games, and have a good time. When it comes to experiences, none get more real than when the Barnetts stay for dinner in the cafeteria at the Dream Center, sharing a meal with the mission's clients. After they eat their own dinner, they get on the line and serve others. Matthew puts his children on the team that serves dessert.

Sometimes Mia and Caden go out with Dream Center crews on deliveries, taking food to the needy, and the lessons they learn are vast, their father said. It's not unusual for Mia to give some of her own toys to children she meets while helping her parents. "I want them to know that's the way life should be lived, that outreach is who we are, not something we have to think about," Matthew explained. "The most exciting time they have is going to the cafeteria and working and serving. It's a life-shaping experience. We don't shield them, we throw them right in the middle of everything. They know the people by name, and they're the guys who just came out from under a bridge."

ABOUT THE BARNETT FAMILY

THEIR CHURCH: Angelus Temple and the Dream Center, Los Angeles, California

DENOMINATION: The Foursquare Church

ATTENDANCE: 5,000 people attend weekly services at Angelus Temple; many more attend services at the Dream Center.

THEIR ROLES: Matthew Barnett is senior pastor and Caroline Barnett is associate pastor; Matthew Barnett is the cofounder (with his father, Tommy Barnett) of the Dream Center.

THEIR FAMILY: The Barnetts have two children: daughter Mia and son Caden.

COMMUNITY OUTREACH: The Dream Center is the community mission arm of the Barnetts' ministry, providing food, clothing, shelter, rehabilitation, job training, and religious services to 40,000 people monthly with the aid of hundreds of volunteers.

ON THE NATIONAL STAGE: The Barnetts have helped start dozens of Dream Centers all over the United States and around the world. Matthew Barnett is a frequent speaker at churches and faith-based conferences, including Promise Keepers and Hillsong.

READ MORE: Matthew Barnett is the author of the *New York Times* best seller *The Cause Within You* and *The Church That Never Sleeps*. To learn more about the Barnetts, Angelus Temple, and the Dream Center, go to angelustemple.org, dreamcenter.org, or matthewbarnett.com.

Caroline's Favorite Basic Side Salad

·······································{ Serves 4 }·······································

This salad is so simple that you can pair it with any entrée, at lunch or at dinner. You can make it your own by adding your family's favorite fresh vegetables. The vinaigrette will give you more dressing than you need, but it will keep in the refrigerator, tightly covered, for up to two weeks. Let it come to room temperature before using. To add extra flavor and a little crunch, you can lightly toast the pine nuts in a small skillet over medium heat. Let them cool completely before adding them to the salad.

1 pound mixed baby salad greens

⅓ cup grape tomatoes

1 medium English cucumber, skin on, diced into ½-inch cubes

¼ cup balsamic vinegar

¾ cup extra-virgin olive oil

Kosher salt

Fresh coarsely ground black pepper

Parmigiano-Reggiano cheese, for shaving

¼ cup pine nuts

Toss the baby greens with the tomatoes and cucumber. Set aside.

Place the balsamic vinegar in a small bowl. While whisking, gradually drizzle the olive oil into the bowl in a thin stream until it emulsifies. Season to taste with kosher salt and coarsely ground black pepper.

Toss the salad with as much or as little of the dressing as you like. Using a potato peeler, shave some Parmigiano-Reggiano pieces on top of the salad, then finish with the pine nuts.

Whole Roasted Chicken

{ Serves 4 to 6 }

Curry is a favorite seasoning of Matthew Barnett's, so it's no surprise that this is his favorite chicken recipe. Caroline likes to roast it with root vegetables such as onions, potatoes, and carrots, but shallots, parsnips, and turnips work well, too.

1 whole chicken

½ teaspoon salt

½ teaspoon freshly ground black pepper

1 lemon, quartered

1 head of garlic

2 tablespoons extra-virgin olive oil

½ teaspoon Lawry's Seasoned Salt

1 teaspoon Madras curry powder, or more as desired (see Note)

½ teaspoon paprika

2 small onions, peeled and quartered

8 to 12 red-skinned potatoes

1 pound carrots, cut into 3-inch pieces

Preheat the oven to 425°F.

Empty the cavity of the chicken and rinse it with cool water. Sprinkle the cavity with the salt and pepper, then insert the lemon quarters.

Cut the garlic head across the top to expose the flesh, but keep the head intact. Place the entire head of garlic into the chicken's cavity.

Tie the legs together with kitchen twine, then place the chicken in a roasting pan. Coat the outside with the olive oil, then sprinkle with the seasoned salt, curry powder, and paprika. Place the chicken in a large roasting pan with the onions, potatoes, and carrots around it.

Place the pan in the oven and bake for 90 minutes, basting the chicken with its juices about halfway through. The chicken is done when an instant-read thermometer inserted in the thickest part of the breast (away from any bone) reaches 165°F.

Remove from the oven, cover with aluminum foil, and let rest for 5 to 10 minutes before transferring to a platter to slice and serve.

{ NOTE }

Curry powder can be spicy, so if you're not used to eating foods with it, start by cutting the amount in half and adjust to taste in the future.

Rack of Lamb

{ Serves 4 }

The Barnetts' menu is heavily influenced by their Swedish heritage, and one entrée they eat regularly is this classic rack of lamb. They use this sugar-salt-pepper seasoning combination on steaks, too.

1 lamb rib roast (6 to 8 ribs)

1 tablespoon packed light brown sugar

1 tablespoon kosher salt

1 tablespoon coarsely ground black pepper

Preheat the oven to 400°F. Let the meat sit out for at least 10 minutes to bring it to room temperature before cooking.

In a small bowl, whisk together the brown sugar, salt, and pepper. Coat the lamb with the seasoning and rub it in enough that it will stay on the meat during cooking.

Heat an ovenproof cast-iron skillet over medium heat and sear the meat for 3 to 4 minutes on each side. Transfer the skillet to the oven and roast for 20 minutes for medium doneness (see Note).

Remove from the oven, cover with foil, and allow to sit for at least 10 minutes before cutting the rack into individual lamb chops.

{ NOTE }

Test for doneness with a meat thermometer—just don't let it touch the bone: 115° to 120°F produces medium rare; 120° to 125°F produces medium.

Scalloped Potatoes

{ Serves 8 }

Caroline Barnett makes scalloped potatoes two ways, with and without onions. If she opts for onionless potatoes, she uses fresh thyme and rosemary to create a flavorful side dish.

2 tablespoons butter

2 to 2½ pounds Yukon Gold potatoes

Salt

Freshly ground black pepper

1 small onion, pureed (optional)

1 teaspoon finely chopped fresh thyme (optional)

1 teaspoon finely chopped fresh rosemary (optional)

2 to 2½ cups heavy whipping cream

Preheat the oven to 400°F. Butter a 2-quart baking dish with 1 tablespoon of the butter.

Use a mandoline or food processor to slice the potatoes thinly.

Place two thin layers of the potatoes in the bottom of the baking dish, sprinkling each with salt and pepper. Sprinkle the pureed onion over the top of the potatoes, or add the thyme and rosemary. Then add two more layers of the potatoes, sprinkling each with salt and pepper.

Pour the cream over the potatoes until it just reaches the top of the potatoes. Make sure there is at least 1 inch to spare in the baking dish so the cream doesn't bubble over into the oven. Top with a few pats of the remaining 1 tablespoon of butter and bake for about 1 hour.

Remove the dish from the oven and allow the potatoes to cool for about 15 minutes before serving.

Creamed Mushrooms

{ Serves 6 to 8 }

Caroline Barnett says this is a great make-ahead dish that tastes better as it develops. The onion will caramelize and give this dish a slightly sweet edge.

10 ounces baby bella mushrooms

1 tablespoon butter

3 tablespoons extra-virgin olive oil

1 yellow onion, sliced thinly

Salt

Freshly ground black pepper

2 cloves minced garlic

½ cup dry sherry or white wine

1 tablespoon fresh thyme, or 1 teaspoon dried

½ cup heavy cream

Wipe off the mushrooms with a wet paper towel. Slice and set aside.

Melt the butter and oil in a large skillet over medium-high heat. Add the onion and a little salt and pepper and sauté for about 3 minutes, or until the onion begins to get tender.

Add the garlic and sauté for about 1 minute more, then add the mushrooms and a little more salt and pepper.

Stir the mixture and let it sauté until the mushrooms release their liquids. The liquids should have mostly evaporated after about 10 minutes; then add the sherry and thyme and stir.

After the liquid has reduced and thickened, add the cream and season to taste with salt and pepper. Cook for 2 additional minutes and serve hot.

Chewy Chocolate Cookies
{ Makes 4 dozen cookies }

Caroline Barnett says that this is her husband's favorite chocolate cookie. It's a rich treat with a fudgy, brownie-like flavor and texture, soft inside, and with just the right amount of crunch outside. If you look for similar recipes online you'll see that it's been widely adapted to suit individual tastes: add walnuts or pecans, chocolate or peanut butter chips, or even sandwich some ice cream between two cookies to make it your own.

2 cups all-purpose flour

¾ cup Dutch-processed cocoa powder

1 teaspoon baking soda

½ teaspoon salt

1¼ cups (2½ sticks) unsalted butter, at room temperature

2 cups sugar

2 teaspoons vanilla extract

2 large eggs

Preheat the oven to 350°F. Line two baking sheets with parchment paper.

In a large bowl, sift together the flour, cocoa powder, baking soda, and salt. Set aside.

Using an electric hand or standing mixer, cream together the butter, sugar, and vanilla. Then add the eggs one at a time and continue beating until the mixture is light and fluffy, about 2 minutes. Reduce the mixer speed to low and gradually add the dry ingredients.

Cover the bowl with plastic wrap and chill until firm, at least 1 hour. (Don't rush the dough. If it's not sufficiently chilled, the cookie dough will spread out all over the pan during baking.)

Roll the dough into 1-inch balls and place them on the prepared baking sheets about 1½ inches apart.

Bake for about 8 minutes. Allow the cookies to cool on the baking sheets for a few minutes, then transfer them to a wire rack to cool completely.

{ NOTE }

If you like your cookies with even more crunch, dip one side of the cookie dough balls into granulated sugar, then place them on the baking sheet sugar side up to bake.

CHAPTER ELEVEN

Rev. Dr. Jim and Barb
Dixon

·········{ Cherry Hills Community Church ✑ Highlands Ranch, Colorado }·········

Dear Jesus,
Thank You for blessing our family,
our marriage, our children, and our grandchildren.
Thank You for Your grace and mercy on us.
Please use this food to keep us healthy,
that we might serve You in the years to come.
We love You and we thank You
for Your protection and provision.
In Your great name, amen.

BREAKING BREAD WITH JOY AND CELEBRATION

When Barb Dixon was a teenager, her parents often hosted visiting missionaries who'd come through town to report on what the church's donations had enabled them to do and rally members to give more.

"It was all about missions at our church," said Barb of her upbringing in Los Angeles. "We'd invite them for a Sunday meal. We'd have a roast in the oven with a timer on. For us kids, it was fun to have people over; they'd have kids and always had good stories to tell."

Perhaps the most popular of the visitors were Paul and John Schlener, missionaries who, with their wives and children, set up a post along the Amazon River in Brazil in the 1950s. The village eventually was named for them: the Port of Two Brothers. "They had amazing stories about living on the Amazon, how they had to fight off the natives, were almost killed, and fought off huge insects and snakes," Barb recalled. "They'd take canoes up and down the river. It was a wild life, completely the opposite of living in and growing up in L.A." She may have loved hearing their adventurous tales, but she also liked that the missionaries had sons—one of whom was a very cute boy who was her age. "I loved it when they came to our house to eat," she said.

Her mother, Ruth Batts, prepared what many moms did then: pot roast with potatoes and vegetables in a Dutch oven. When they got home from church she'd prepare a salad, cut up some fruit, and call it a meal. When Barb became a young wife and mother, she prepared the same meals she learned from her mother.

Not only did Barb's family entertain visiting missionaries, for a time they also were part of a lay missionary effort. Through the week, Ruth and Marvin Batts raised their three girls—Barb was the oldest—in Los Angeles. On weekends, they'd head north to a migrant worker camp in Bakersfield, where they lived in a trailer and ministered to poor farmworkers from the small church her dad had built. "We really didn't have any way, other than ice in a cooler, to keep anything cold, so our dinners were Cheerios with warm milk," she said. "We collected food at home and gave it out to the migrants. We'd take clothes, just like we do here in the inner city in Denver, helping people with food and clothing and shelter."

When Barb was young, her mother came down with debilitating rheumatoid arthritis, and the family's mission work ended. She and her sisters had to do more around the house, and once Barb got through seventh-grade home economics, she stepped up for kitchen duty. "Mom's specialty was spaghetti, which I loved, and it was the first thing I wanted if I was ever sick," Barb recalled. "It was even better the second day, after the flavors all soaked into the pasta."

"Some people eat to live and others live to eat. It was an unspoken motto in our home [growing up] that we ate just to survive," she said with a laugh. "On Friday nights, my parents had a family party, and we had things that we didn't have during the week, like potato chips and that onion dip you made with soup mix, and we had pop. Chips, dip, and pop—that was our family party on Friday nights."

Her family may not have had elaborate meals or rich traditions, but most everything they did revolved around their faith. They always ate dinner together, followed by Bible readings. And to make sure his daughters were listening, Marvin Batts stopped every now and then and asked them to repeat his last sentence. When the lesson was over, they had a family prayer. She remembers that her parents were so strict that she and her sisters weren't allowed to dance. To attend a high school dance, Barb had to sneak out of the house.

After college, Barb lived in Pasadena, California, with four other young women. Two of the girls had graduated from Westmont College, where Jim Dixon was a student at Fuller Theological Seminary, and they had invited Jim and his roommate to a party for Barb's birthday in October 1970. When Barb and Jim met, there was a spark, but it took Jim until Thanksgiving to muster the courage to ask her for a date. When he did, she turned him down—she already had plans to go skiing with her family. So he invited her to a Christmas party. They were engaged by Easter and married the following August. To-day, they live in Highlands Ranch, Colorado, where Jim has been senior pastor at Cherry Hills Community Church since its opening in 1982.

As she got to know her in-laws, Barb learned about a whole new way of cooking and eating. Jim's mother, Nina Dixon, was a great cook and an even better baker. To this day, Barb Dixon's freezer almost always has bags of cookies from two of her mother-in-law's best recipes: chocolate chip cookies and Ranger Cookies.

Jim, the youngest of three boys, grew up in the La Cañada Flintridge suburb of Los Angeles and attended Hollywood Presbyterian Church. All three Dixon boys grew up to work in ministry. Gary Dixon pastored a Presbyterian church and Greg Dixon does mission work in Central America, but both now live in the Denver area and attend Cherry Hills Community Church.

When the Dixon boys were growing up, dinner was a family event. Their mother inquired about schoolwork and friends, and the type A brothers all had plenty to say. "We were three boys, so sometimes we'd talk about girls." Jim laughed. "There was always conversation at the table. It was generally a happy time and my brothers and I have great memories."

Jim said his mother was a wonderful cook, but the dishes he remembers most were her desserts: pies, cobblers, and cookies. "My mom was a Missouri farm girl who was a great cook. She made a gooseberry cobbler and boysenberry cobbler that were something else. The crust alone . . . I'm sure they were very high in calories, but, boy, what a treat."

Barb Dixon said she and her sisters-in-law initially tried their hand at Nina Dixon's recipes but gave up. They just couldn't replicate her crust for pies and cobblers. When Jim's mother made big meals, the daughters-in-law cleaned up afterward. "We never contributed to the cooking because she was so good at it," Barb said. "Her sons would rave about her food. They'd go on and on . . . and once in a while I'd think, 'Well what am I, chopped liver?' But her claim to fame was her cooking skills."

After more than forty years of marriage, the Dixons have cut back on the sweets they eat, so when Barb bakes or wants to experiment with a new recipe, she'll take the dish in for the office staff at the church. "They'll eat anything," she quipped.

When their daughter, Heather, and son, Drew, were born, the Dixons knew they wanted to continue many of the family dinner traditions they grew up with, but they wanted to do them their way. Sometimes she'd declare it was "every man for himself night" and they'd clean the fridge of leftovers.

"I tried to make things that they liked. I made sure they didn't have a whole lot of stuff they had to gag down," Barb said, remembering the peas her parents forced her to eat. "I tried to make it tasty and fun."

The book of Acts describes how people met in homes and broke bread together with great joy, Jim said. So that's what he and Barb set out to do: create a life at home that was fun, yet meaningful. Their meals were a time for good conversation, whether they were at home or in a restaurant. "I would have to say that in terms of our family life, those evening meals were the glue that, relationally, held us all together," Jim explained. "I felt God used that to keep us close as a family, not just close to each other but close to Him. Our walk with Christ is part of everything we do and everything we say. Our conversations always include discussions about the Lord."

Jim made a point of spending time with his children doing things they liked. On "father-kid night," he'd take Heather and Drew to a movie and then to dinner to discuss the movie. "It was a great chance for me to talk about matters of theology and morality in the context of the movie," Jim said. "Barb joined us sometimes, too, but we did it every week. The kids looked forward to that, and they would pick the restaurant."

When Jim was growing up, his father built a swimming pool and set up a basketball court so he could watch his boys play. He remembers the smile on his father's face from those days and wanted to re-create that for his children. Although Heather wasn't athletic, Drew enjoyed playing golf. "We watched football together and played golf. Four hours in a cart was an amazing father-son experience," he said.

Among the values the Dixons instilled in their children was that of loving and being loved. "There are biblical values for the things you shouldn't do, but far more than that are the wonderful things you're supposed to do . . ." he said. "We'd discuss what the loving thing to do was; learning to love, which isn't easy. Some people are hard to love; sometimes we're hard to love. We are very concerned with loving God and people."

Now that Drew and Heather are grown and have families of their own, mealtime is simpler for Barb and Jim Dixon. Sundays are, too.

Barb always considered Jim's calling her own, so she accompanies him whenever he represents the church and does what she can to help him prepare for Sundays when he preaches at three services. They get up early and as he goes over his sermons one final time, Barb makes a hearty breakfast of eggs and sausage or bacon. They pause for a prayer time before leaving for the church.

After services they stop in the church coffee shop and head to his office to relax. Sometimes they go out for lunch and take their children and grandchildren. And, if it's football season, they head home to watch the Denver Broncos on television.

Holidays and birthdays now are often the times when everyone gathers in the Dixon home. At Christmas, Barb makes a big breakfast and gets out her barista machine, and they all open their gifts and drink lattes and cappuccino. Later in the day, the extended family gathers at Heather's home for a big dinner. "Last Christmas, we had one of those turduckens. It was interesting, but we all decided that would be the last one," Barb laughed.

She loves doting on her grandchildren, kids who are decidedly not picky eaters and will eat fruit and vegetables—even broccoli. "I call my granddaughters the fruitarians," she said. "When I babysit, I make sure I have blueberries and strawberries. They're very high-energy kids, especially the girls."

When the Dixons are home in the evening, they watch TV and make a bowl of popcorn. They toss in Hot Tamales candies to get a taste of both salty and sweet. Jim Dixon is starting to cook, and the first thing he wants to master is a good guacamole. "We decided that when we retire we may take a cooking class together," Barb said. "Maybe a dance class, too."

ABOUT THE DIXON FAMILY

THEIR CHURCH: Cherry Hills Community Church, Highlands Ranch, Colorado

DENOMINATION: Nondenominational

ATTENDANCE: 13,000 members

THEIR ROLES: Jim Dixon is the founding and senior pastor.

THEIR FAMILY: The Dixons have two children: daughter Heather Lowe (husband Chris) and son Drew (wife Rachel). They have three grandchildren: Abigail, Nina, and Dixon.

COMMUNITY OUTREACH: Cherry Hills has many outreach initiatives in the Denver area as well as around the world. They work with other Denver-area churches and ministries to help the poor and homeless. More than 3,500 people from the church have been on mission trips, from medical/dental trips to building homes and water facilities for villages in Africa and elsewhere.

ON THE NATIONAL STAGE: Jim Dixon is involved in leadership training for ministers, including the annual Global Leadership Summit. He also serves on the board of directors of Colorado Christian University.

READ MORE: Jim Dixon is the author of *Last Things Revealed: Hope for Life and the Everafter*. To learn more about the Dixons and Cherry Hills Community Church, go to chcc.org.

Avocado and Shrimp Fettuccine

{ Serves 4 }

Barb Dixon found this pasta recipe in one of her favorite recipe books, the Junior League of Denver's *Crème de Colorado Cookbook*. White wine and garlic deepen the cream sauce's rich flavor, and the red pepper flakes give it an extra kick.

4 tablespoons (½ stick) butter

1 teaspoon minced garlic

2 tablespoons minced fresh parsley

½ pound shrimp, peeled and deveined

2 tablespoons white wine

½ cup heavy cream

¼ cup freshly grated Parmesan cheese

Pinch of crushed red pepper flakes

¼ teaspoon salt

⅛ teaspoon freshly ground black pepper

9 ounces fettuccine, cooked al dente, drained, and kept warm

1 avocado, peeled, pitted, and cubed

In a large skillet, heat 1 tablespoon of the butter over medium heat. Add the minced garlic and cook for 1 minute. Add the parsley, shrimp, and white wine and cook for 2 minutes, stirring constantly, until the shrimp turn pink. Do not overcook. Transfer the shrimp mixture to a small bowl and set aside.

In the same skillet, melt the remaining 3 tablespoons of butter. Reduce the heat to low and add the cream, Parmesan, and red pepper flakes; cook for 3 minutes, stirring constantly, until the cheese melts and the sauce is smooth. Stir in the salt and black pepper.

To serve, place the warm fettuccine in a serving dish (see Note). Add the shrimp mixture, sauce, and avocado and toss gently to coat the pasta with the sauce.

{ NOTE }

To help the pasta stay warm during dinner, heat the serving dish in the oven before putting the cooked fettuccine in it.

Spaghetti Pie

{ Serves 6 }

This kid-friendly casserole is easy to assemble, and a great make-ahead dish. Barb Dixon found this recipe in her Junior League of Denver *Colorado Cache Cookbook*.

½ pound angel hair pasta

2 large eggs, beaten

½ cup finely grated
   Parmesan cheese

2 tablespoons olive oil

1 onion, diced

1 cup sour cream

1 pound Italian sausage

1 jar (at least 16 ounces)
   spaghetti sauce

2 cups shredded Cheddar
   cheese

Preheat the oven to 375°F. Spray a 9-inch round, glass baking dish with nonstick cooking spray.

Cook the pasta according to the package instructions. Mix the cooked pasta with the eggs and Parmesan until combined. Spread the pasta mixture over the bottom of the prepared pan.

Heat the oil in a medium-size pan over low heat. Add the onion and sauté until translucent. Mix the cooked onion into the sour cream and layer the mixture over the pasta.

Cook the sausage in a sauté pan until it's no longer pink, then stir in the spaghetti sauce. Pour the sausage mixture on top of the sour cream layer. Top with the Cheddar cheese.

Cover the pie with foil and bake for 30 minutes. Uncover and bake 15 minutes more to lightly brown the cheese. Allow to cool for a few minutes before serving.

Spinach Frittata

This veggie-filled frittata makes a special breakfast entrée, but don't be afraid of trying it for lighter dinner fare. It's easy to make and can satisfy even the heartiest of appetites.

3 tablespoons light olive oil

½ cup thinly sliced white onion

10 large eggs

½ cup milk

1 teaspoon salt

½ teaspoon freshly ground black pepper

¼ teaspoon minced fresh sweet basil

1½ cups coarsely chopped fresh spinach leaves

2 tablespoons minced fresh parsley

2 medium-size tomatoes, firm and ripe, sliced thinly

½ cup crumbled feta cheese

6 kalamata olives, pitted and sliced thinly

Preheat the oven to 350°F.

In an 8- or 9-inch cast-iron skillet, heat the oil and sauté the onion, stirring until soft, about 3 minutes.

In a large bowl, beat the eggs and milk with a wire whisk, then fold in the salt, pepper, basil, spinach, and parsley. Turn the egg mixture into the skillet with the onion and cook over low heat, lifting from the bottom with a spatula as the eggs set.

After 3 minutes, arrange the tomatoes, crumbled feta, and olive slices on top of the frittata, then bake until firmly set and slightly browned, about 15 minutes.

Serve from the skillet while hot.

Ranger Cookies

Jim Dixon grew up eating his grandmother's Ranger Cookies, a recipe that's been around since the 1930s. Variations abound, some including chocolate chips or chopped nuts. For a contemporary update on this not-too-sweet cookie, try adding a cup of white chocolate chips when you add the cereals and coconut.

1 cup (2 sticks) butter, at room temperature

1 cup granulated sugar

1 cup firmly packed brown sugar

2 large eggs

1 teaspoon vanilla extract

2 cups all-purpose flour

1 teaspoon baking soda

½ teaspoon baking powder

½ teaspoon salt

2 cups old-fashioned oats

2 cups crispy rice cereal

1 cup shredded sweetened coconut

Preheat the oven to 350°F. Grease a baking sheet.

In a large bowl, cream the butter and sugars until light and fluffy. Add the eggs and vanilla, mixing until the dough is smooth.

In a separate bowl, sift together the flour, baking soda, baking powder, and salt. Add the dry ingredients to the butter mixture a little at a time, stirring until they're thoroughly combined. Add the oats, cereal, and coconut and stir until incorporated.

Roll the dough into balls and flatten with a fork on the prepared baking sheet. Bake for 10 to 12 minutes, or until a light golden color.

14-Karat Cake
with Cream Cheese Frosting

{ Serves 12 }

This carrot cake recipe has been shared by bakers for decades. Barb Dixon doesn't remember exactly where she got it, but she remembers the raves she's heard every time she makes it. This recipe produces a dense yet moist cake that's perfected by a generous portion of cream cheese frosting.

CAKE

2 cups all-purpose flour

2 teaspoons baking powder

1½ teaspoons baking soda

1 teaspoon salt

2 teaspoons ground cinnamon

2 cups sugar

1½ cups vegetable oil

4 large eggs

2 cups grated raw carrots

1 (8¼-ounce) can crushed pineapple, drained

½ cup chopped pecans

FROSTING

1 (8-ounce) package cream cheese, softened

½ cup (1 stick) butter or margarine, at room temperature

1 teaspoon vanilla extract

3¾ cups confectioners' sugar, sifted

Preheat the oven to 350°F. Grease and flour two 8-inch round cake pans or one 9 by 13-inch baking pan.

MAKE THE CAKE: Sift together the flour, baking powder, baking soda, salt, and cinnamon in a large bowl. Add the sugar, oil, and eggs and mix well. Stir in the carrots, pineapple, and pecans until mixed well.

Pour the batter into the prepared pans and bake until a toothpick inserted into the center comes out clean, 30 to 35 minutes for 8-inch round cake pans or 35 to 40 minutes for a 9 by 13-inch pan. Remove the cake from the oven and allow it to cool completely.

MAKE THE FROSTING: Beat the cream cheese and butter in a large bowl until they're thoroughly blended. Add the vanilla and continue to beat. Gradually add the confectioners' sugar and beat until the sugar is incorporated and the frosting is fluffy. Frost the cooled cake.

Pecan Pie

{ *Serves 6 to 8* }

Karo syrup gives this pie its glossy texture, and its creamy filling offsets the generous layer of crunchy pecans. Barb Dixon says she's been making this pecan pie for holidays and other special dinners since the mid-1970s.

3 large eggs

½ cup firmly packed
  brown sugar

1 tablespoon granulated
  sugar

1 cup light Karo syrup

½ cup dark Karo syrup

2 tablespoons butter,
  melted

⅛ teaspoon salt

1½ tablespoons all-
  purpose flour

1 teaspoon vanilla extract

1½ cups pecans

1 (9-inch) unbaked pie
  shell

Preheat the oven to 325°F.

In a large bowl, beat the eggs slightly. Add the sugars and Karo syrups. Continue beating, adding the remaining ingredients, finishing with the pecans.

Pour the pie filling into the unbaked pie shell. Bake for 40 minutes, or until set. Remove from the oven and allow to cool to room temperature before serving.

CHAPTER TWELVE

Rev. George and Joan

Foreman

God, wake me up daily, let me always grow as a person.
Give me the strength to work so I can provide for my family.
Let me learn to make new friends, always mindful of my old friends.
Keep a place in my Heart for my mom, dad, and
all of my loved ones who have gone on to the other world.

Keep Jesus Christ as my friend so I can be reminded that
no one is first or last in Your eyes.

Let me look into the mirror daily and see Your blessings, never
complaining about the things I don't have and understanding that
salvation is what makes us truly rich—a free gift from above.
Let me always see envy and jealousy as a waste,
for no one of us has anything that can be taken with
us when we leave this life.

Let me serve You. Paul had his chance, Peter, and the rest;
now let me. Let me be myself.
Amen.

SUNDAY, A DAY FOR WORSHIP AND FELLOWSHIP

George Foreman was just a boy during the late 1950s in Houston's Fifth Ward. It was a difficult time and a dangerous place for a black boy, the fifth of seven children his mother could barely feed. She was a short-order cook who occasionally could bring home leftover food from the restaurant where she worked. A simple sandwich or piece of meat would have to be divided several ways, each child getting a tasty morsel, but none ever knowing the feeling of a full belly.

But young George knew that not all children were hungry. He knew others had mothers—and fathers, too—who were home at night and led a different family life. He hid outside their homes, watching from his uncomfortable position in their often scratchy bushes, swatting away mosquitoes in the hot, humid air. He saw mothers, fathers, and children gathered around kitchen tables, bowls heaped with steaming potatoes and other vegetables, and platters oozing with savory meats. They clasped their hands for a short prayer and then waited for their plates to be filled.

He could close his eyes and feel the crunch of fried chicken or the fatty creaminess of mashed potatoes in his mouth. In his dreams—desperate hopes, actually—the kindhearted mothers or strong, caring fathers would invite him in to share the meal. He believed that if they saw the hunger in his eyes, they could understand the longing in his heart and then they would invite in the boy who was starving both for food and for a sense of belonging. But they never did. Not one person ever invited him in or brought a plate of food out to him. Not one ever made a single gesture of kindness to the boy who had little more than the clothes on his back.

"That's what I mean when I say there's not enough kindness in this world," said George, who lives in Houston with his wife, Mary ("Joan"), and several of their ten children. "Growing up was hard for me; far too many times people weren't kind to me. Kindness is very important to me—simple kindness."

In a few years, he grew into an intimidating figure. As a teen he became a mugger and a thief, the only way he knew how to survive. He disliked school and couldn't get a job to earn money for food or to help his mother, but he knew how to steal it.

Baby boomers and older Americans remember George Foreman as a hulking figure in the boxing ring, who earned a gold medal at the 1968 Olympics and then at age twenty-four won his first heavyweight championship in 1973 against Joe Frazier. George later became a hero to the middle-aged when he won his final championship belt at the age of forty-four, when he beat twenty-six-year-old Michael Moore. A younger generation knows him as an entrepreneur, the pitch man for the George Foreman Lean, Mean Grilling Machine. During the 1990s, the countertop grills sold by the millions, and they're still popular today. He's a pop culture figure, too, having competed on Season 7 of Donald Trump's *The Apprentice* and getting his own reality show, *Family Foreman*, which aired six episodes in the summer of 2008. He's hosted *Saturday Night Live*, guest judged on *American Inventor*, and appeared as an animated character on *King of the Hill*. Over the years, he's become one of America's most familiar faces, appearing on virtually every talk show from Jay Leno to David Letterman, as well as those of Jimmy Kimmel, Tyra Banks, and Tavis Smiley.

As familiar as his face may be here and around the world, there's one side of George that's often overlooked: his role as pastor of the Church of the Lord Jesus Christ in Houston, Texas. It was in 1977 that George became a born-again Christian, after a religious experience in his dressing room after losing a twelve-round decision to Jimmy Young in a boxing match in Puerto Rico.

Some years later, he opened his Houston church and a nearby youth boxing center that serves as a ministry to young men. George is a deeply religious man; prayer and Bible study are a fundamental part of his day. His small church is in a working-class neighborhood just north of the city's downtown. Its paved parking lot is neatly landscaped; on Sunday its blacktop is covered with late-model SUVs, Lexuses, BMWs, Mercedes-Benzes, and other luxury cars. Sometimes there's even a white stretch limo parked at the side of the church. The four services a week—evening services on Wednesday, Saturday, and Sunday, plus a Sunday morning service—find two hundred or so fitting comfortably in the traditional wooden pews arranged amphitheater style. Plain white walls are angled to focus a visitor's attention on what's up front: a pulpit and immersion baptism pool.

From that pulpit George does his work. There's no choir, but small groups sing at the start of services. Sometimes George picks up an acoustic guitar, strumming and singing along. The melodies are simple and familiar, his voice sincere. He reads from the Bible, punctuating points from his sermon with chapter and verse so his congregation can follow along. George is neither a speechwriter nor an academic; his style is more informal storyteller. He relates tales from his career in boxing or his life at home as husband, father, and grandfather. His messages urge congregants to be good friends, spouses, and parents; to be responsible at home and at work.

He talks about the Job Corps program that pushed him into boxing as a youth and heads nod in agreement at the idea that adults need to find something special to cultivate in each child. He tells a story about trying to get his son to eat salad, and parents chuckle that even a four-time heavyweight champion of the world can't demand respect for a plate of lettuce. Love and respect between a husband and wife are a recurring theme in his sermons, drawing laughter and "Amens" from women in the audience.

"If you really want to find meaning in life, look at your family," George said. "That's your life. You can achieve a lot and obtain wealth, but if you have no family, you're missing the boat."

On the rest of his Sunday, from breakfast through bedtime, Rev. George Foreman prefers simply to be called "Dad"—oh, and don't forget "Grandpa."

"I'm a preacher, and I live this thing," said George of his faith and the family dynamic. "They hear me in church four services a week, so when we get together on Sunday afternoon, we just want to be a family."

George, Joan, and their children—five boys, all named George (more on that later), and five girls—seem to be in constant contact: they call and text, and they connect on Facebook. George mentors son George III, nicknamed "Monk," a Rice University graduate who has launched a boxing career of his own. Another son, George IV, works for his dad and seems ever present. Other children grew up, went to college, and moved away for careers of their own. Some eventually moved back to Houston.

Parenting is an intentional and essential part of George's life. He may have five young granddaughters, but he also has a ten-year-old son at home. "You know you're a success as a parent when a child says, 'Let me live my own life,'" George said. Wife Joan shies away from the media and interview requests. She prefers a low-key role so she can travel around town unnoticed.

To understand George Foreman as a parent, you first have to understand his view of his children. He's gotten much attention for naming all of his sons "George," and loves to explain why he did it. Despite his own rough-and-tumble childhood—or perhaps because of it—George decided many years ago that he wanted any sons he had to become the man he had become: someone who works hard, loves honestly, provides for his family, and earns respect. "I tell my sons that we are all George Foreman, so what any one of us does reflects on all of the others," he explained. "When one of us is in trouble, we are all in trouble. When one of us does well, we all do well."

The discipline and work ethic George taught by example clearly took hold in his sons—and his daughters, too.

"Dad has such a good reputation, and he expects all of us to maintain that reputation," said George IV, "Big Wheel," a student at Texas Southern University. "I always get a smile when I introduce myself to people. Always. How many people can say, 'My dad has left every person in the country with a smile on his face'?"

College life and jobs may take the Foremans' children to other states, but on just about any Sunday they'll find at least half of them in Houston. And anyone who's in town on Sundays is expected to go to church and get together for a big family meal. Big Wheel lives in one of his parents' homes near the church, and they all refer to it as the "church house." Any family members who are up and about early drop in there for breakfast before the ten a.m. service.

By eleven thirty a.m. or so, George Foreman finds himself at the door to his church, shaking hands with each and every person as they leave. Then the Foremans head back to the church house for the afternoon. Children and grandchildren are always there, but often so are George and Joan's extended family. Brothers and sisters, nieces and nephews, and family friends drop in, too. Many bring casual clothes to change into for the day; those who forget often raid Big Wheel's closet.

Meals are full of family favorites, meaning that everyone will find a favorite "something" on the table. For one son it may be pancakes; for another it's pork chops or steaks. Everyone loves salads, or so Dad says.

What's George's favorite? "I just love fixing the food," he said, noting that he still sticks to his boxing regimen of fish or chicken and veggies. "Two weeks ago, I made roast pork with lots of herbs. Everybody piles around and Joan slices it."

"The best Sunday dinners are built around a big piece of meat—a big prime rib roast, pork shoulder, or spareribs. I season them well, but I don't use salt," he continued. "We have lots of salads and lots of vegetables, too. We make simple salads and everyone adds on their favorite fixings and dressings. And a big pot of beans, too. Joan's are the best; she learned to make them from my mom."

Joan Foreman said that she usually leaves sugar off the menu and salt and fat out of most dishes. That big pot of beans George likes is made with turkey instead of ham hocks, the way his mother made it. If she makes hot water corn bread—another family favorite—the kids add a sprinkle of sea salt and a little butter on their own. Desserts don't play a big role in their Sunday dinners, though George says they occasionally will buy pies to finish things off.

There's much more to the Foreman family all-day feast than church and food. There's the company. They all love to talk about sports, current events, and what's happening in their lives. There are movies to critique, music to dissect. "Growing up, you'd sit and listen to everyone," said Big Wheel. "It's a major day when you get to voice your own opinion at Sunday dinner."

Because Big Wheel lives in the church house, his Sundays are hectic—and he loves every minute of it. "Sunday is such a big day. The TV is usually on; the sport depends on the time of year," he said. "During football season, there's a lot of smack talk because we're a family of ten kids and six Georges—and every George has a favorite team." Big Wheel said his current favorite team is the New York Jets because its coach, Rex Ryan, gave a shout-out to his dad during the 2009 playoffs when he called his team "the George Foreman of the playoffs." When basketball season rolls around, the Foreman daughters are more likely to join in the sports revelry. Not only are they more interested in that sport, but its players and their wives also often show up in pop culture.

George Foreman grins from ear to ear when he talks about the mountains of food he and his wife prepare for their Sunday dinners. The irony of their vastly different childhoods is not lost on them. "I have had rough conversations with my children about the way I lived. I didn't want my kids to be spoiled, but I wanted them to do well," he said. "A friend of mine and I were talking one day about putting his kids in private schools. He didn't want to do it, but his wife thought it was time. He said, 'If our parents could have, they would have given us the best education possible. They just couldn't do it.' Giving children the best start in life and the best education possible isn't spoiling them."

The Foremans' children have grown up with many advantages, but they also rode a bus to public school and did their homework at the kitchen table. For all that goes with having a very famous father, George Foreman's children grew up with an incredibly normal home life. "Both of my parents grew up in vastly different situations than mine," said Big Wheel. They've given us an odd sense of humility that is difficult for people to understand and hard for us to put into words."

What he can articulate is that he grew up watching his father work very hard for everything they have, a work ethic that continues to this day. "It took me twenty years to realize my dad was famous," Big Wheel continued. "All I saw was the hard work.

I remember when I was eight or nine, I saw my dad come in from a long training run. It had been raining and he was wet and muddy. I don't remember the fights or the titles; I remember the hard work that went into training."

Joan Foreman grew up in poverty in Saint Lucia, but the Caribbean island is dotted with fruit trees and surrounded by the ocean, so fresh fruit and fish were always available. The couple met when George went to the island on business. He had recently gone through a divorce and needed someone to help care for his four children. She came to Houston to be his nanny, but when her six-month stay was up, Foreman realized he didn't want her to leave. So he took her to a jewelry store in a shopping mall, bought a ring, and got down on one knee to propose on the spot.

Their parental roles are fairly traditional. While George travels a good deal for business on weekdays, he's almost always home on weekends for church. Joan maintains the home front and was the one to keep the children on task when it came to school and other activities.

As much hardship as they have to look back on, the Foremans prefer to look ahead, George said. They want their children to understand that life can be hard, but any hardship can be overcome. And while they have taught their children to have the same Christian values, they also want them to be individuals.

Foreman jokes that sometimes they're a little too much alike, and a little too much like him. "Sometimes the little things they say and do, I'm not happy about because it's like they've all been cloned," he said. "They act, look, and behave exactly alike. I've done a horrible job of cloning them. They're all headstrong . . . like me."

Foreman loves to tell stories about his youngest, ten-year-old George VI, who goes by the nickname "Joe." The family owns a home in Saint Lucia, where Joan grew up. When they visited there once, they stopped at a beachside restaurant before heading to their home. Foreman described Joe as a no-nonsense boy who loves nature and animals of all kinds. So Foreman picked up a small hermit crab from the beach and took it up to their home to surprise Joe. "Joe was upset and said, 'We've got to set him free,'" recalled Foreman, telling the story with dramatic gestures. "He made me go back to the beach where I picked him up to set him free. He made a big production out of it and gave a big speech. I videotaped the whole thing."

Foreman laughs when he tells this story, because of the sensitive nature of his youngest son, and because of his tendency to want to make decisions for his children as they get older. He has to remind himself to just let them be who they are. "I think you have to let children develop from within themselves. Joe makes us love animals."

Of all the things Foreman teaches his children, one of the most important is forgiveness: "Forgiveness is the subtle thread that binds both love and friendship," said Foreman. "If you're not willing to forgive, can you wake up without your spouse, child, or friend?"

Foreman claims to be neither a perfect person nor a perfect father. In his own relationship with his children, he knows they might be cross with him at one time or another. The solution is never to walk away. "To walk through the front door, my children have a lot of forgiveness for me, and I for them," said Foreman. "They forgive me for trying to be too much of a father."

When a Sunday afternoon turns to evening and the Foremans are all talked out, they clean up the kitchen and put away leftovers—if there are any. Then they change back into their church clothes and pile into cars to return to the Church of Our Lord Jesus Christ for an evening service. "I'm afraid they're going to fall asleep during my sermon because they're so full of food," George Foreman said with a laugh. "I try to keep the sermon short so it's over before the snoring starts."

ABOUT THE FOREMAN FAMILY

THEIR CHURCH: The Church of the Lord Jesus Christ, Houston, Texas

DENOMINATION: Nondenominational

ATTENDANCE: 500 attend weekly services.

HIS ROLE: George Foreman is pastor.

THEIR FAMILY: George and Joan Foreman have ten children: sons George Jr., George III "Monk," George IV "Big Wheel," George V "Red," and George VI "Joe," as well as daughters Michi, Freeda George, Georgetta, Natalie, and Leola.

COMMUNITY OUTREACH: George Foreman started the George Foreman Youth and Community Center in 1984, and many Houston teens have found focus and discipline through its boxing program. The program itself inspired him to return to the ring—leading to his final heavyweight title at the age of forty-four—when the boxer needed to raise money to support the center.

ON THE NATIONAL STAGE: Foreman is known by different generations for different things. He is an Olympic gold medalist, boxing legend, and four-time heavyweight champion of the world. Gen Xers know him as the frontman for the George Foreman Lean Mean Grilling Machine empire. And Gen Yers know him as a reality TV participant on Season 7 of Donald Trump's *Celebrity Apprentice*, as well as the center-piece of his own reality show, *Family Foreman*.

READ MORE: Foreman is the author of several books, including *Fatherhood by George*, *Going the Extra Smile*, *God in My Corner*, and *George Foreman's Guide to Life*. To learn more about the Foremans and the Church of Our Lord Jesus Christ, go to georgeforeman.com.

Herb-Roasted Salmon

{ Serves 4 }

Since George Foreman's days as a boxer, he learned to eat a clean diet of chicken, fish, and fresh produce to build muscle and avoid fat. To this day he avoids red meat, and salmon, halibut, tuna, or another fish are his go-to entrées. Lemon juice and herbs season this dish to perfection.

¼ cup olive oil

Juice of 1 lemon

1 teaspoon freshly ground black pepper

1 teaspoon garlic powder

½ teaspoon onion powder

4 salmon steaks, or a 1½- to 2-pound salmon fillet

Pour the olive oil into a shallow baking dish. Add the lemon juice, pepper, and garlic and onion powders and stir to distribute the seasonings through the oil.

Add the salmon, skin side down if using a fillet. Then turn the salmon so that the flesh side is down and press into the seasoned oil to coat. Cover the dish with plastic wrap and refrigerate for 1 hour or more to marinate.

When you're ready to roast the fish, preheat the oven to a low broil. Remove the plastic wrap from the baking dish, turn the salmon flesh side up, and cook for 10 to 12 minutes.

Steamed Vegetables

{ Serves 4 to 6 }

The Foremans keep it simple in their everyday cooking. In addition to maintaining the low-cal, low-sodium regimen of a boxer trying to "make weight," the family prefers the natural flavors of fresh produce.

2 teaspoons olive oil
2 cups water
1 cup broccoli florets
1 cup chopped asparagus
1 cup cauliflower florets

Place the olive oil and water in the bottom of a medium-size saucepan and heat over medium heat.

When the water begins to boil, insert a steamer tray and add the vegetables. Steam for 8 minutes. Serve immediately.

Berry-Nut Salad
with Lemon Vinaigrette

{ Serves 6 to 8 }

The Foreman family loves salads. When everyone's together, a plain salad is almost always served and each person adds cheese, veggies, dressings, or other goodies according to individual taste. George Foreman likes his with berries and nuts for their healthy antioxidant value.

VINAIGRETTE

¼ cup balsamic vinegar

1 cup olive oil

½ cup freshly squeezed lemon juice

1 teaspoon prepared mustard

SALAD

8 cups mixed baby salad greens

1 cup cherry tomatoes

1 cup blackberries or blueberries

½ cup walnuts

½ cup green grapes

8 green olives, pitted and sliced

MAKE THE VINAIGRETTE: In a small bowl or shaker bottle, combine the vinaigrette ingredients. Stir or shake until combined. Set aside or refrigerate until ready to use.

MAKE THE SALAD: Wash the salad greens and place them into a large salad bowl. Add the cherry tomatoes, sliced in half if they're larger, berries, nuts, grapes, and olives. Top with the vinaigrette, toss, and serve.

Hot Water Corn Bread

{ Serves 10 }

These corn bread patties cook quickly for a crunchy exterior and a warm, creamy interior. Add a little butter while they're still hot, for a decadent treat. Joan Foreman makes them without salt to suit George's taste, and you can, too, if you're on a salt-free diet.

1 cup peanut oil
1½ cups white cornmeal
½ teaspoon salt
1 cup water

Pour the peanut oil into a deep skillet over medium heat.

While the oil is heating, combine the cornmeal and salt in a large bowl.

Heat the water to boiling, then add it to the cornmeal mixture. Stir well and let the cornmeal thicken to the consistency of warm cereal. (If it's too thin, add more cornmeal 1 tablespoon at a time.)

The oil should be between 325° and 365°F for deep frying. If you don't have a kitchen thermometer to monitor the temperature, insert the end of a wooden spoon into the hot oil; if the oil starts to bubble up, it's ready.

Drop spoonfuls of the cornmeal mixture into the hot oil and, with the back of the spoon, spread it into the shape of a patty. Cook for about 1 minute and then flip, continuing to cook for 1 more minute on the other side. If the oil gets too hot, adjust the temperature down.

Vegetable Soup

{ Serves 8 }

Joan Foreman buys veggies in bulk and then chops them up and freezes them in resealable plastic bags. That makes for an easy supper soup she can have on the table in minutes. Because George eats such a clean diet, his soup is free of fat and sodium, but any family can adapt this to their taste by adding their favorite seasonings, broth, and protein.

1 small squash, chopped (2 cups)

1 small zucchini, chopped (2 cups)

1 cup chopped celery

⅓ cup packed chopped fresh parsley

1 cup chopped carrots

2 cups shredded cabbage

1 bunch green onions, white parts only, chopped

8 cups water

1 teaspoon seasoned salt

Place the vegetables in a large stockpot. Add water and seasoned salt and cook over medium heat until the vegetables are tender but not overcooked, about 20 minutes.

Beans and Rice

{ Serves 10 to 12 }

George Foreman likes beans the way his mother made them. His wife Joan is from St. Lucia and wasn't used to cooking beans when they met, so he asked his mother to teach her to make them, Texas style. To suit George's healthier lifestyle, Joan makes these beans with turkey necks instead of ham hocks. If you don't mind the extra fat, go ahead and prepare them with ham hocks for an authentic, smoky flavor. If you like them spicy, try adding two teaspoons of cumin, plus a teaspoon each of black pepper and cayenne pepper.

1 pound dried red beans

6 cups water

1 medium-size onion, cut in half

3 cloves garlic, minced

1½ cups chopped red, green, yellow, or orange bell peppers

3 pounds fresh turkey necks

2 teaspoons salt

4 cups cooked brown rice, for serving

Wash and rinse the beans, then put them in a large stockpot with 6 cups of water and let sit overnight in the refrigerator.

The next day, place the pot with beans and water—don't change the water—on the stove over medium heat. Add the onion, garlic, bell peppers, turkey necks, and salt and boil for 1 hour. Remove the turkey necks, chop them up, and pick the meat out. Return the turkey meat to the beans.

Reduce the heat to low and simmer for 3 hours. Serve with brown rice.

CHAPTER THIRTEEN

Pastors Ron and Hope

Carpenter

·······{ Redemption World Outreach Center ⌘ Greenville, South Carolina }·······

Father, thank You for this food we are about to receive
as nourishment for our bodies. Thank You for Your
promise to take sickness and disease out of our midst.
For this and all of Your goodness, we pray in Jesus' name.
Amen.

A COUNTRY-STYLE MENU WITH SOUTHERN CHARM

Ron Carpenter Jr. grew up in the "middle of nowhere" in South Carolina. Sundays revolved around church—his father was a Pentecostal preacher—and that meant three services, with a midday meal in a diner in town, sandwiched between morning and evening services. It was always Southern comfort food—fried meats with gravy, cooked vegetables, and old-fashioned desserts—similar to what he ate at home weeknights in Possum Kingdom, South Carolina, but on this day his mother got the day off from cooking.

When he headed off to Emmanuel College—a Franklin Springs, Georgia, school affiliated with the International Pentecostal Holiness Church (IPHC)—it was to play basketball and be on the lookout for pretty girls, not to prepare for his father's profession.

Sometime during his freshman year there, a group of high school seniors came to campus and Ron was among the students called to show the visitors what life was like at this small, liberal arts Bible college. "I spotted Hope all the way across a huge auditorium," said the still-smitten Ron of the woman he's now been married to for twenty-three years. "Later that night I found her, knelt down on one knee, and asked her for her name."

Hope thought the lanky blond athlete was awfully cute and, of course, she told him who she was. She watched him play basketball the next day, and for the remainder of her senior year in high school they talked occasionally by phone. The two started dating when Hope enrolled at Emmanuel the next fall, and in a year they were engaged.

After they married, they began two important projects: starting a family and starting Redemption World Outreach Center, an IPHC-affiliated church that has grown from a congregation of three people to a sprawling, multicultural ministry with more than fifteen thousand members in Greenville, South Carolina. (Ron's father, Ron Carpenter Sr., is the presiding bishop of the IPHC, located in Oklahoma.) Their family now includes three teenagers, sons Chase and Chaz and daughter Chanlin, and, now, their first grandchild.

"Possum Kingdom was a triangle where about twelve people lived, and my family was one of them," Ron said with a laugh. "If you were to come to this church, it's a huge joke that the pastor is from Possum Kingdom."

Hope Carpenter's family came from a town that was larger, but not by much. She's from Calhoun Falls, South Carolina, in nearby Abbeville County, with little more than two thousand people and a single stoplight for city streets. Both of her parents, Sandy and

Judy Hilley, worked, and her mother would come home each evening and prepare a meat and three vegetables for her family for supper. And when she was old enough to learn her way around the kitchen, it was Hope's turn to help. "My mom cooked every single day, and when I turned fifteen, Mom said, 'Okay, I want dinner on the table at five o'clock every night, no ifs, ands, or buts about it,'" Hope recalls. "Needless to say, those early family dinners weren't so good."

She's only half joking. "My mom made the best biscuits. I remember the first time I made them, they were so hard that my brother threw one on the floor and it made a sound like *clunk*," she said. "Mom made those homemade buttered biscuits every morning when I was growing up, and I remember I'd be sitting there at the table eating them, and my mom would be saying, "Hope, get up, you've got to get to the bus stop.""

But she watched her mother cook when she could, and she learned. Today she's much more skilled at making biscuits, but says she'd rather eat second helpings at dinner instead of breads or even desserts. Still, Hope declares that she reserves the right to go to a Hardee's fast-food restaurant once a week for her biscuit fix.

Then and now, fresh vegetables factor heavily in the Carpenter family menu. Hope said she grew up with a huge garden in the backyard in the summer and their table would be filled with fried okra or squash and cucumbers soaked in vinegar, seasoned simply with salt and pepper. "I had helped in the kitchen because we always had chores to do. I'd make a cake—it was a box cake—but I'd make it on my own," she said. "Because both of our parents worked, my brother and I had to fend for ourselves. I just figured it out on my own."

When Ron and his sister were kids, breakfast might be a Pop-Tart or a toaster waffle. Lunch consisted of whatever the school cafeteria served. But dinner was a showcase for his mother's skills in the kitchen. "Whether I was seven or seventeen, at suppertime the family ate together, period. Dinner was sacred," Ron said. "It was always country cooking. I don't remember a day we didn't have gravy. Everything a doctor would tell you not to eat was the food we ate every day."

They never had take-out pizza. Pans of lasagna never came out of the oven and a slow cooker filled with a casserole never sat on his mother's kitchen counter. Nan Carpenter fed her children meat and vegetables—and, yes, the gravy that Ron loved—every day. "Everything was garden fresh," Ron said. "My aunts and uncles were farmers in North Carolina. Whenever we visited, they'd fill our trunk with food and fresh vegetables."

He and his father loved the outdoors, so it wasn't unusual for them to bring home wild game or fresh fish for dinner. "We were hunters and fisherman, and if we had a big catch we'd have a big fish fry. Those redneck ways you see on TV? We lived them out," he joked.

The tall, willowy Hope says she's blessed with a healthy metabolism, and Ron still has the athlete's build of his early years. But several years ago, a health problem surprised the family. Ron had gone to the doctor complaining of headaches. After the doctor checked his blood pressure, he had shocking words for the pastor. He explained the nature of high blood pressure. Ron had no real symptoms, had always been a healthy weight and always led an active lifestyle filled with exercise. "It happened when I was thirty-five and was connected to my diet," he said of his high blood pressure diagnosis. "It was a wake-up call."

Initially Ron feared he'd get put on a bland diet in which nothing tasted good. Hope changed the way she prepared the foods they'd always eaten and took gravy off of the menu. Their food is now grilled or roasted—not fried—but it's still pretty good.

The rare exceptions are holidays, when their extended family comes together at Ron and Hope's home, and everyone brings their best dishes. Ron's mother makes her country-style steak with gravy—Ron's favorite. Hope's mother makes biscuits, beans, and maybe a red velvet cake. Hope makes macaroni and cheese, which Ron says no one can come close to matching. "Holidays are awesome because we have our parents, siblings, and their kids over," said Hope. "It's a lot of food. Our holidays revolve around food, with home cooking."

On Sundays now, the Carpenters might eat their midday meal at church in a café that feeds church members between morning services. Evening meals are casual and often involve Ron's manning the grill in the backyard to make burgers or chicken.

On weeknights, Hope emphasizes healthier meats and vegetables, along with other favorites. And, around the table, the time spent together is about focusing on family. "We don't bring church to the table. We try to make it about the moment and what they're going through," Ron said. And because all three Carpenter kids are teenagers, extra seats at the dinner table are always filled. Afterward, they might splash around in the backyard pool or grab a bowl of popcorn and plop onto bean bag chairs to watch movies.

Ron and Hope want to know their children's friends, and they also want their home to feel like a second home to them as well. It's not unusual for any number of friends of their sons and daughter to call the couple Mom and Dad.

"Our church is geared to broken people, so kids don't just see us as a pastor. If they're from a broken home they may see us as Mom or Dad, not just the pastor or pastor's wife," Ron said.

Regardless of who's at the table, it's a time for personal updates. The kids talk about their friends, who's dating whom, and what's going on in school. It's also a time for their kids to spend time with each other, as otherwise they're all with their own friends. But the most crucial lesson, Ron said, is the importance and value of family itself. "Sometimes they think I'm going overboard. We fill our plates, but no one starts eating until we're all at the table," he explained. "I want them to place value on the family blessing, to wait until we're all at the table. It's an old-fashioned tradition I'm trying to keep alive."

Dinner conversation is lively as personalities come through. Chanlin is fifteen and the youngest, but always has something to say. On the other end is seventeen-year-old Chaz, who doesn't talk much unless you ask questions. Their eldest, Chase, is away at college, but holds his own between his talkative sister and quiet brother.

More than anything, Hope wants her children to enjoy the time they spend together. She said that when she was a girl, dinnertime was quiet and more formal, and she and her brother were expected to mind their manners—even though they wanted to relax and tease each other. "We laugh and cut up," Hope said of her family dinners now. "I always thought meals were a time when you should have fun."

Ron simply wants to enjoy his children while they're still home, creating memories from which they can draw when it's time to raise their own families. "We won't have these times forever, so let's enjoy them now. We're more tender to that than we've ever been. My youngest is a freshman in high school, and for the next four years I'm going to milk every moment I can."

ABOUT THE CARPENTER FAMILY

THEIR CHURCH: Redemption World Outreach Center, Greenville, South Carolina

DENOMINATION: International Pentecostal Holiness Church

ATTENDANCE: 10,550 attend weekly services; 15,000 members.

THEIR ROLES: The Carpenters are the founders and senior pastors of RWOC. Hope Carpenter is founder and leader of the church's Women of Hope ministry.

THEIR FAMILY: The Carpenters have three children: sons Chase and Chaz, and daughter Chanlin. They have one grandson.

COMMUNITY OUTREACH: RWOC has many ministries, but one of its most unusual is the Imagine Center, a state-of-the-art gymnasium that offers league sports, group exercise, and personal training, and puts all profits back in the community. The church has many ministries for members of all ages, but works hard to provide job training and employment assistance and other community services to help Greenville residents and church members remain self-sufficient.

ON THE NATIONAL STAGE: RWOC holds the annual Kingdom Transformation leadership conference. The church also founded the Redemption Ministerial Fellowship International, a network of 1,300 churches and ministries around the world.

READ MORE: Ron Carpenter is the author of *The Necessity of an Enemy*. To learn more about the Carpenters and Redemption World Outreach Center, go to rwoc.org or roncarpenter.com.

Slow Cooker Macaroni and Cheese

{ Serves 6 to 8 }

If you like your mac 'n' cheese super creamy and super cheesy, this is the recipe for you. It's a snap to make and can easily be doubled to feed a larger group.

8 ounces macaroni

3 cups grated sharp Cheddar cheese

½ cup (1 stick) butter, melted

2 large eggs

1 (12-ounce) can evaporated milk

1½ cups whole milk

Spray the inside of a slow cooker with nonstick cooking spray.

Bring a large pot of water to a boil. Cook the macaroni in the boiling water for about 10 minutes. Drain the macaroni in a colander and then transfer it to the slow cooker.

Add the cheese to the macaroni and stir. Pour the butter over the macaroni mixture.

In a medium-size bowl, whisk the eggs with both milks, then add the mixture to the macaroni. Stir to incorporate, then cover and cook on LOW for 3 to 4 hours, or until hot and bubbling.

Sunday Pot Roast

{ Serves 8 to 10 }

What busy mother hasn't made this tender, delicious pot roast? The soup mixes save prep time and add plenty of flavor, and the slow cooker does the rest of the magic.

2 tablespoons olive oil

3 to 3½ pounds boneless beef bottom round roast or chuck pot roast

1 (10¾-ounce) can condensed cream of mushroom soup

1 envelope (about 1 ounce) dry onion soup mix

12 or more large red-skinned potatoes

3 cups carrots that have been cut into 2-inch pieces

1 cup celery that has been cut into 2-inch pieces (optional)

Heat the olive oil in a large skillet over medium heat and add the roast. Sear the roast on each side. Transfer the meat to a 4½-quart slow cooker.

In a small bowl, stir together the mushroom soup and dry soup mix. Pour the mixture over the meat in the slow cooker. Top the roast with the potatoes, carrots, and celery, if using.

Cover and cook on LOW for 8 hours, or until the beef is fork tender. Serve on a large platter with the vegetables arranged around the roast.

Asparagus Casserole

{ Serves 6 to 8 }

Even the fussiest eaters won't be able to pass on this hearty side dish: fresh asparagus topped with creamy sauce and cheese and finished with a buttery, crunchy, topping.

2 (15-ounce) cans asparagus, drained well, or 1 pound fresh asparagus, chopped

1 (10¾-ounce) can condensed cream of mushroom soup

8 ounces shredded Cheddar cheese

½ cup (1 stick) butter

1 sleeve buttery or club-style crackers

Preheat the oven to 350°F.

Place the asparagus in the bottom of a casserole dish. Spread the condensed soup across the asparagus and then top it with the shredded cheese.

In a microwave-safe bowl, melt the butter. Crumble the crackers and add to the melted butter, mixing well. Cover the asparagus mixture with the cracker mixture and bake for 25 to 30 minutes, or until the cracker topping is golden brown.

CHAPTER FOURTEEN

Revs. Drs. Floyd and Elaine
Flake

·········{ Greater Allen AME Cathedral ✿ Jamaica, Queens, New York }·········

Almighty God,
it is with gratitude and humility that we gather today
to celebrate our lives and our love. We express our sincere devotion
to You and to the purpose that You have assigned to our time on Earth,
and we pray that obedience and victory will always be our reality.
Bless us, oh Lord, as we seek to do Your will, and please, lead us
down the paths of righteousness for Your name's sake.
Bless the food that we are about to eat, and grant that
health and happiness will follow us all the days of our lives.
In the name of our risen Savior, Jesus Christ, we pray, amen.

A FULL HOUSE, FULL HEARTS

Floyd Flake was just a skinny boy of ten or eleven, but he could still command quite an audience in his parents' backyard. He'd put on his best clothes—those reserved for church or other important occasions—and he'd call his younger sisters to attention. They'd be decked out in their mother's old clothes and shoes from the pile she set aside for them to use to play dress-up.

If any living thing had passed away, Flake and many of his seven siblings felt it ought to have a proper burial. If a creature's soul was to ascend to heaven, the Flake kids would send it on its way in raucous style. Young Floyd would affect his voice just like the preachers he heard on Sunday mornings. He'd gesture with his whole body, arms raised to the sky. His timbre rose and fell in a sing-song cadence, sending his "congregants" into a tizzy of screams, squeals, and laughter, finishing with a rousing "Amen."

"I probably always knew I wanted to be a preacher," said Floyd, who through the years also has been a U.S. congressman, university president, and businessman, all while serving the Greater Allen Cathedral, an African Methodist Episcopal Church in the Jamaica area of Queens, New York, for more than thirty-five years. The church had a healthy membership of fourteen hundred when he started there. His businesslike style and compassionate sermons—with much help from his inspiring wife, Elaine, also an ordained minister—have brought the church's ranks to more than twenty-three thousand through the years.

Floyd grew up in 1950s Houston in the Acres Homes subdivision, built as a place for black families to raise their children. It was near the Garden City Park and Paradise Cemetery, but those were difficult times for African Americans. The park was far from a garden and paradise was hard to imagine.

His father, Robert Flake Sr., always worked two to three jobs and his mother, Rosie Lee Flake, was busy caring for her large family. Rosie Flake had given birth to thirteen children, but Floyd was just one of eight who survived childhood.

"On Sundays we got up early for Sunday school and Daddy would take us. He always washed the car first—Daddy would not go to church in a dirty car," Floyd said of his family's participation at Ward Chapel AME Church. Early on, their father didn't stay at church with them, but when he became a churchgoer he went in the mornings and accompanied Floyd to evening services, too.

Church often lasted until one or two p.m., then they went home to eat and relax. Sunday was special in the Flake household. It was the one day of the week that his father didn't work. His mother would prepare a huge meal—usually getting started on Saturday—and friends and family often dropped in. "We would go out and get peaches and she'd make a cobbler," Floyd remembered. "We had cake every Sunday—coconut, pineapple. Rarely did we not have dessert."

His mother was a great cook, he said, and she prepared a big pot of beans, plus rice and corn bread every day. He was on the track team in high school and his teammates often came home with him, and they'd all chow down.

By the time he was in high school, his future vocation was apparent. Jewel Houston, a teacher from his school, had taken him under her wing. She was in charge of youth ministry for the district, and on Sundays she'd drive him to guest preach at churches in and near the city. The day he informed his family that he'd felt called to the ministry, his older sister looked straight at him and said, "Now you'll never have a girlfriend."

After high school Floyd headed off to Wilberforce University in Ohio. He earned a bachelor's degree there and later studied business at Northeastern University and religion at United Theological Seminary in Dayton, Ohio. He tried his hand at social work and even took a job as a marketing analyst. He thrived in academia, working as dean of students at Boston University. It was when he was attending church—Saint Paul AME Church in Cambridge, Massachusetts—that a beautiful young school teacher, Elaine McCollins, caught his eye. They dated for a while and eventually married. They're now parents to two daughters and two sons: Aliya, Nailah, Robert, and Harold.

Elaine's family background is a stark contrast to Floyd's. Where Floyd was one of many children, Elaine was an only child in Memphis, Tennessee. Both of her parents worked, so her maternal grandmother, Addie White, took care of her until she was old enough to go to school. "I liked that grandmother best . . . she was the better cook," Elaine said with a laugh. Her grandmother cooked for her every day, and she never tired of her favorite meal: spaghetti with collard greens and corn bread.

On Sundays they always went to church and then headed straight to her grandmother's. By the time they got dinner ready it was usually midafternoon. "For me, Sunday was the day we visited uncles and aunts. We'd sit out on the porch at my grandmother's. Sunday was always a family day," she said.

Her grandmother may have been an incredible cook, but so was Elaine's mother. When she visits her daughter and son-in-law in New York, she rules the kitchen. "She's eight-six years old and still is meticulous about the kitchen. She doesn't like anybody in the kitchen," Floyd said.

In 1976, Floyd found himself taking over the pulpit of the historic Greater Allen AME Cathedral of New York. His congregation already seemed large, fourteen hundred members. But he was determined to deliver on the vision of self-help established by the denomination's eighteenth-century founder, Richard Allen, after whom the cathedral is named.

Floyd inspires his church's members to better education, economic empowerment, and social and political action by, quite literally, practicing what he preaches. The Flakes helped the church open a private school and start social and commercial ventures that have made the church the largest private-sector employer in Queens. As Floyd gained influence in the community for his church work, he gained notice politically. He was elected to the U.S. House of Representatives in 1986 and served New York's Sixth Congressional District for eleven years, focusing on business and urban revitalization, before leaving Congress to devote more time to the church.

Along the way, the Flakes and their children made many friends, including two sisters. The women each had a child who died young: one lost her son to leukemia; the other lost her daughter in a shooting by her classmate. The sisters already were members at Greater Allen, but in their grief they turned even more to God and to their pastors. They started babysitting for the Flakes' children and soon were considered part of the family.

As the Flakes built their own Sunday dinner tradition, these women certainly were part of it. In fact, on the first Sunday of each month, the two sisters host the family dinner. "They make real Southern food: fried chicken, ribs, coleslaw, potato salad, macaroni and cheese, and collard greens," said Elaine. "It's wonderful."

When the Flakes' children were younger, the family would get home and "have church all over again" as Floyd described it. They had so many activities that they often ate in restaurants after church.

Eventually, the family started eating at home again. "The kids are older now, and we don't have to run to dance classes or ball games," Floyd said. "It's more fun to be at home now. We can all kick our shoes off, take naps, and kick back."

Their Sunday routine is still pretty busy: Floyd and Elaine leave the house by 5:45 a.m. for services at 6:30, 8:30, and 11:15. Rarely do they leave the church before 2:00 p.m.

To make meal preparation easier, Floyd gets the meats ready the night before. Sometimes Elaine prepares a roast. They get a little help with side dishes from a housekeeper.

"The children come over every Sunday, along with a few stragglers from the church who follow us home," Floyd said. "We always have guests. We take people home; we feed everyone," Elaine added.

They see their children—and their granddaughter—at morning services, of course, but there's always a lot to talk about in the Flake household. Son Robert works for a state senator and a daughter works for the state controller, so discussions of current events and politics are unavoidable. Then there are sports. During football season they head downstairs to watch the NFL on TV, but they follow basketball, too.

The kitchen counters might be laden with food, but no one fills a plate until everyone stands and holds hands to say grace. They might eat in the dining room if they have special company, but it feels more like family when they all spread out: Some sit around the kitchen table, and others sit on the couch to watch sports on TV. It's all very informal, and feels just right to them.

Elaine and Floyd said that they cook to please everyone, so it's not unusual for their kids to call to tell them what they'd like for dinner: fish, roast, steak, or ribs. Sometimes they'll make all of it. Their children and friends often stay until six or seven p.m. and most take leftovers home with them.

However the day goes, Floyd said that his goal has always been to capture the sense of family he knew growing up in Texas. "We're open, just like my mother was," he said. "It's a sense of family and tradition, and we love being with one another."

ABOUT THE FLAKE FAMILY

THEIR CHURCH: Greater Allen AME Cathedral, Jamaica, Queens, New York

DENOMINATION: African Methodist Episcopal

ATTENDANCE: More than 23,000 are members.

THEIR ROLES: Floyd Flake is senior pastor; Elaine Flake is co-pastor.

THEIR FAMILY: The Flakes have four children: daughters Aliya and Nailah, and sons Robert and Harold. They have one granddaughter.

COMMUNITY OUTREACH: The Flakes have started many programs to help their congregation and the community surrounding their church. In addition to a school for kindergarten and first graders, Greater Allen has a shelter for battered women and a prison ministry. The church also has commercial ventures that provide employment.

ON THE NATIONAL STAGE: While a minister, Floyd Flake served eleven years as a U.S. congressman, and for several years served as president of Wilberforce University. He has served on boards for the President's Commission on Excellence in Special Education, the Fannie Mae Foundation, the Princeton Review, the New York City Investment Fund Civic Capital Corporation, the Federal Deposit Insurance Corporation Advisory Committee on Banking Policy, and the Bank of America National Advisory Board.

READ MORE: Floyd Flake is the author of *African American Church Management Handbook* and *The Way of the Bootstrapper: Nine Action Steps for Achieving Your Dreams*. Elaine Flake is the author of *God in Her Midst*. Together they coauthored *Practical Virtues: Everyday Values and Devotions for African American Families*. To learn more about Floyd and Elaine Flake and the Greater Allen AME Cathedral, go to allencathedral.org.

Pot Roast

·····························{ Serves 10 or more }·····························

On Sunday mornings, ovens across America are turned on for this eagerly antici-pated pot roast. Home cooks return a few hours later to find a satisfying, tender roast and enough savory mushroom sauce to fill any gravy boat. This forgiving recipe can be adapted to any family's tastes, and is sure to have your children asking for seconds.

1 (3 to 5-pound) beef pot roast

2 teaspoons seasoned salt

1 tablespoon (total) of your favorite herb or herbs

1 can (10¾-ounce) golden mushroom soup

Preheat the oven to 450° to 500°F.

Season the beef with the salt and herbs. Place in a deep baking dish, then roast for 15 to 20 minutes, or until the meat is browned and crisp on the edges.

Remove the roast from the oven and reduce the oven temperature to 325°F.

While the oven temperature is adjusting, spoon the mushroom soup on top of the meat. Cover the roasting pan with a lid or aluminum foil and return it to the oven. Bake for 2½ to 3 hours, basting once or twice if desired, until the roast is fork tender.

Squash Casserole

{ Serves 8 }

You won't have trouble getting your family to eat their vegetables if you prepare this side dish. Try it when your garden is bursting with summer zucchini and yellow squash, and you'll be hooked on this nutritious casserole.

2 pounds squash
1 carrot, grated
½ cup (1 stick) butter
1 medium-size onion, chopped
1 (10¾-ounce) can cream of chicken soup
1 cup sour cream
1 cup grated mild or sharp Cheddar cheese
1 cup stuffing mix

Preheat the oven to 350°F. Grease a 9 by 13-inch pan.

Chop the squash into 1-inch pieces. Place the pieces in a steamer insert in a large saucepan with a little water in the bottom and steam over medium-high heat until fork tender. Transfer to a large bowl and add the grated carrot.

Melt the butter in a medium-size saucepan over medium heat. Add the onion and sauté until translucent, about 5 minutes. Add the soup, sour cream, and cheese and stir. When the mixture is blended and starts to bubble, pour it over the squash. Add the stuffing mix and stir to incorporate.

Transfer the casserole to the prepared pan and bake for 30 minutes, or until bubbling and golden on top.

Broccoli Casserole

{ Serves 8 }

If you like to make big meals and have a few side dishes you can preassemble, then bake just before serving, this recipe should be in your Sunday arsenal. If you'd like to dress it up, mix ½ cup of panko bread crumbs with 2 tablespoons of melted butter and sprinkle over the top before baking.

1 (10-ounce) box of frozen chopped broccoli, or 3 cups chopped fresh broccoli

1½ cups cooked rice

1 small onion, chopped

¼ cup (½ stick) butter

4 ounces pasteurized cheese product, such as Velveeta

1 (10¾-ounce) can cream of mushroom soup

Preheat the oven to 350°F. Grease a 2-quart casserole dish.

Cook the broccoli as directed on its package. For fresh broccoli, place in a steamer insert in a medium-size saucepan with a little water in the bottom and steam over medium-high heat until fork tender. Drain and set aside in a large mixing bowl with the cooked rice.

In a saucepan over medium heat, sauté the onion in the butter until translucent, 4 to 5 minutes. Reduce the heat and add the cheese to the pan. When it's melted, mix in the soup and cook until the mixture is bubbling. Add the onion mixture to the broccoli and rice and stir until incorporated.

Pour the casserole mixture into the prepared baking dish and bake for 25 minutes, or until hot and bubbling.

Pound Cake

{ Serves 12 }

The name for this cake lies in its origins. Earliest recipes—from the 1700s—called for a pound each of butter, sugar, eggs, and flour. We do the measuring for you for this dense, moist cake that's a year-round Flake family favorite. It is just as good eaten plain as it is dressed up with seasonal fruits.

3¾ cups cake flour

1 pound (4 sticks) butter

3¾ cups confectioners' sugar

1 teaspoon vanilla extract

1 teaspoon almond extract

6 large eggs

GLAZE

1¼ cups confectioners' sugar, sifted

3 tablespoons milk

Preheat the oven to 325°F. Grease and flour a 10-inch tube pan or two 9-inch loaf pans.

Sift the flour; set aside.

In a stand mixture or with an electric hand mixer, beat the butter and sugar at medium speed until fluffy. Add the vanilla and almond extracts and mix well. Add the eggs and flour alternately to the butter mixture.

Pour the batter into the prepared pan and bake for 50 to 60 minutes, or until a toothpick inserted into the center comes out clean.

MAKE THE GLAZE: Place the confectioners' sugar in a small bowl. Stir in the milk one tablespoon at a time until it reaches the consistency you like. Drizzle the glaze over the cooled pound cake and let set before serving.

Thanks

Writing *Sunday Dinners* has been a labor of love, and taking it from concept to printed product has brought support from and hard work by many people.

First, I have to thank my sisters, Cindy Niemantsverdriet and Patty Rigdon, with whom I have so many shared experiences from our childhood. As spouses, nieces, and nephews entered the picture, they all shaped our family experience, at the dinner table and otherwise. My husband, Steve Cowen, and his family taught me much about what it means to open your heart and your home to others.

I've shared meals with many people, but my closest friends and frequent recipe "tasters" Kathy and Shane Richolson, Randy and Jim Lane, Maryellen and Mark Martin, and Denise and Al Dylla deserve special attention. They've become my second family in Houston and have all believed in the book from the first interview.

My agent Blythe Daniel has never waivered in her enthusiasm and support for the book throughout the process of going from proposal to publisher. She has taught me much about patience and professionalism.

My team at Andrews McMeel—editor Lane Butler, art director Tim Lynch, designer Holly Ogden, publicist Emily Farris, and others who had a hand in making it exactly what we wanted it to be—deserve a standing ovation for their efforts. Lane guided the book with a smart but gentle hand, Holly and Tim shaped its look with their keen attention to detail, and Emily has been creative and tireless in her efforts.

My friends and colleagues at the *Houston Chronicle*—Jeff Cohen, Kyrie O'Connor, Melissa Aguilar, Greg Morago, and many more—have provided so much support and enthusiasm along the way.

And, of course, I have to thank all of the families who agreed to share their stories with me for this book: Pastors Victoria and Joel Osteen, Rev. Dr. Ed and Jo Beth Young, Bishop T. D. and Serita Jakes, Rev. Kirbyjon and Pastor Suzette Caldwell, Rev. George and Joan Foreman, Pastors Matthew and Caroline Barnett, Rev. Mike and Jeannie Glenn, Rev. Dr. Jim and Barb Dixon, Rev. Randy and Rozanne Frazee, Pastors Samuel and Eva Rodriguez, Pastors Hope and Ron Carpenter, Revs. Drs. Floyd and Elaine Flake, and Rev. Martin Lam Nguyen, CSC. They are all kind and generous ambassadors for great food, strong families, and deep faith. Thank you all.

METRIC CONVERSION FORMULAS

To Convert	Multiply
Ounces to grams	Ounces by 28.35
Pounds to kilograms	Pounds by 0.454
Teaspoons to milliliters	Teaspoons by 4.93
Tablespoons to milliliters	Tablespoons by 14.79
Fluid ounces to milliliters	Fluid ounces by 29.57
Cups to milliliters	Cups by 236.59
Cups to liters	Cups by 0.236
Pints to liters	Pints by 0.473
Quarts to liters	Quarts by 0.946
Gallons to liters	Gallons by 3.785
Inches to centimeters	Inches by 2.54

APPROXIMATE METRIC EQUIVALENTS

Volume

¼ teaspoon	1 milliliter
½ teaspoon	2.5 milliliters
¾ teaspoon	4 milliliters
1 teaspoon	5 milliliters
1¼ teaspoons	6 milliliters
1½ teaspoons	7.5 milliliters
1¾ teaspoons	8.5 milliliters
2 teaspoons	10 milliliters
1 tablespoon (½ fluid ounce)	15 milliliters
2 tablespoons (1 fluid ounce)	30 milliliters
¼ cup	60 milliliters
⅓ cup	80 milliliters
½ cup (4 fluid ounces)	120 milliliters
⅔ cup	160 milliliters
¾ cup	180 milliliters
1 cup (8 fluid ounces)	240 milliliters
1¼ cups	300 milliliters
1½ cups (12 fluid ounces)	360 milliliters
1⅔ cups	400 milliliters
2 cups (1 pint)	460 milliliters
3 cups	700 milliliters
4 cups (1 quart)	0.95 liter
1 quart plus ¼ cup	1 liter
4 quarts (1 gallon)	3.8 liters

Weight

¼ ounce	7 grams
½ ounce	14 grams
¾ ounce	21 grams
1 ounce	28 grams
1¼ ounces	35 grams
1½ ounces	42.5 grams
1⅔ ounces	45 grams
2 ounces	57 grams
3 ounces	85 grams
4 ounces (¼ pound)	113 grams
5 ounces	142 grams
6 ounces	170 grams
7 ounces	198 grams
8 ounces (½ pound)	227 grams
16 ounces (1 pound)	454 grams
35.25 ounces (2.2 pounds)	1 kilogram

Length

⅛ inch	3 millimeters
¼ inch	6 millimeters
½ inch	1.25 centimeters
1 inch	2.5 centimeters
2 inches	5 centimeters
2½ inches	6 centimeters
4 inches	10 centimeters
5 inches	13 centimeters
6 inches	15.25 centimeters
12 inches (1 foot)	30 centimeters

COMMON INGREDIENTS AND THEIR APPROXIMATE EQUIVALENTS

1 cup uncooked rice = 225 grams
1 cup all-purpose flour = 140 grams
1 stick butter (4 ounces • ½ cup • 8 tablespoons) = 110 grams
1 cup butter (8 ounces • 2 sticks • 16 tablespoons) = 220 grams
1 cup brown sugar, firmly packed = 225 grams
1 cup granulated sugar = 200 grams

OVEN TEMPERATURES

To convert Fahrenheit to Celsius, subtract 32 from Fahrenheit, multiply the result by 5, then divide by 9.

Description	Fahrenheit	Celsius	British Gas Mark
Very cool	200°	95°	0
Very cool	225°	110°	¼
Very cool	250°	120°	½
Cool	275°	135°	1
Cool	300°	150°	2
Warm	325°	165°	3
Moderate	350°	175°	4
Moderately hot	375°	190°	5
Fairly hot	400°	200°	6
Hot	425°	220°	7
Very hot	450°	230°	8
Very hot	475°	245°	9

Information compiled from a variety of sources, including *Recipes into Type* by Joan Whitman and Dolores Simon (Newton, MA: Biscuit Books, 2000); *The New Food Lover's Companion* by Sharon Tyler Herbst (Hauppauge, NY: Barron's, 1995); and *Rosemary Brown's Big Kitchen Instruction Book* (Kansas City, MO: Andrews McMeel, 1998).